Read all of the books in this exciting,
action-packed biography series!

Hank Aaron

Muhammad Ali

Lance Armstrong

David Beckham

Barry Bonds

Roberto Clemente

Sasha Cohen

Joe DiMaggio

Tim Duncan

Dale Earnhardt Jr.

Doug Flutie

Lou Gehrig

Wayne Gretzky

Derek Jeter

Sandy Koufax

Michelle Kwan

Mickey Mantle

Jesse Owens

Alex Rodriguez

Wilma Rudolph

Annika Sorenstam

Ichiro Suzuki

Jim Thorpe

Tiger Woods

SPORTS HEROES AND LEGENDS™

Wayne Gretzky

by Matt Doeden

Twenty-First Century Books/Minneapolis

For Mom & Dad, for tying my skates

Twenty-First Century Books
A division of Lerner Publishing Group, Inc.
241 First Avenue North
Minneapolis, MN 55401 U.S.A.

Website address: www.lernerbooks.com

Cover photograph:
© Bruce Bennett Studios/Getty Images

Library of Congress Cataloging-in-Publication Data

Doeden, Matt.
    Wayne Gretzky / by Matt Doeden.
        p.   cm. — (Sports heroes and legends)
    Includes bibliographical references and index.
    ISBN 978-0-8225-7165-0 (lib. bdg. : alk. paper)
        1. Gretzky, Wayne, 1961—-Juvenile literature. 2. Hockey players—
    Canada—Biography—Juvenile literature. I. Title.
    GV848.5.G73D64 2008
    796.962092—dc22 [B]   2006039086

Manufactured in the United States of America
1 2 3 4 5 6 – JR – 13 12 11 10 09 08

Contents

Prologue

Fifty Goals in Thirty-Nine Games

When Wayne Gretzky skated onto the ice in Philadelphia, Pennsylvania, on December 30, 1981, every hockey fan knew that the star center was on his way to shattering yet another National Hockey League (NHL) record. He was playing the Philadelphia Flyers in his thirty-ninth game of the season, and he'd entered it having already scored forty-five goals. He seemed assured of becoming the fastest player to reach fifty goals in a season. The previous record of fifty goals in fifty games had been set by Maurice Richard thirty-six years earlier and tied by Mike Bossy just the year before.

Wayne, just twenty years old, and his Edmonton Oilers were one of the NHL's exciting young teams. Wayne was already the league's reigning Most Valuable Player (MVP), and his scoring was the talk of the league. It was only a matter of time before he broke the record. But surely, he would need another week or two to break it. Even if he scored one goal each game, fans had plenty of time before the record would fall.

In the first period, Wayne's teammate Paul Coffey fired a hard shot that sailed wide left of the Philadelphia Flyer goal. The puck bounced straight to Wayne, and he flicked it past goaltender Pete Peeters with a quick wrist shot. A few minutes later, Wayne controlled the puck with Edmonton on a four-on-two break (four Edmonton players skating toward the Philadelphia goal against only two Flyer players). Instead of passing, as he'd usually do in that situation, Wayne reached back and fired a hard shot from twenty feet away. The slap shot surprised Peeters, who could only watch as it sailed by.

In the second period, Wayne stayed hot. He used his speed to break out behind the Flyers' defense. One-on-one, Peeters stood no chance, not against hockey's best player. Wayne calmly fired a shot over the goalie's right shoulder. The goal gave him a hat trick—three goals in one game. Suddenly, the record seemed within reach. His season total had climbed to forty-eight goals.

In the third period, Wayne crept even closer. With fifteen minutes remaining in the game, he controlled the puck about twenty feet from the net. With a quick, tight motion, he pushed the puck to the side of his defender. Then he reached across his own body and lifted a shot that sailed into the net. *Goal number forty-nine!*

The Philadelphia crowd was going wild. "When I got to forty-nine, that's when I realized that this was something really special," Wayne later said.

Wayne was determined to break the record that night. But that wasn't the only reason he wanted to score. The game was still close. The Oilers were clinging to a slim 6–5 lead. A goal wouldn't just be a record breaker, it would also help to ensure an important win for Edmonton.

For the next ten minutes, the Flyers clamped down on Wayne. He had three shots, but Peeters stopped them all. Finally, with the clock running down, the Flyers pulled their goaltender to get an extra skater (a team may have a total of six players on the ice).

With just ten seconds remaining, Oiler goalie Grant Fuhr had the puck. As Wayne skated as fast as he could toward the Flyer zone, Fuhr passed the puck to winger Glenn Anderson at center ice. Anderson then flipped it over to Wayne, who was all by himself. The puck hit Wayne's stick with three seconds on the clock.

A Flyer defender was charging, desperately trying to get in Wayne's way. But Wayne wasn't about to give him time—not with an empty net to shoot at. He slapped the puck forward. As the clock ticked down to one, the puck came to rest at the back of the net. *Goal!* Wayne had done it—his five goals gave him fifty for the year. He'd done it in just thirty-nine games, shattering the old record by eleven games.

Mark Messier led Wayne's teammates to the Flyers' zone, where they mobbed the star center. Even the Philadelphia crowd was going nuts. Their team had lost the game, but the fans knew that they'd just witnessed hockey history. They cheered Wayne as he skated off the ice.

Back in the locker room, Wayne wanted to do only one thing—call his dad. Because his parents lived in Canada and couldn't get most of Wayne's games on television, they waited for his phone call each night to find out how the Oilers had done.

"I did it, Dad! I did it," Wayne told Walter Gretzky, aware that his father had no way of knowing how the game had turned out.

Walter's response to his son was simple. "What took you so long?"

Chapter One

Hockey Prodigy

Wayne Douglas Gretzky, it seemed, was born to play hockey. When his parents, Walter and Phyllis, brought their first child into the world on January 26, 1961, the weather in Brantford, Ontario, Canada, was cold and icy. Wayne was born into a family of hockey fans and into a country that adores the sport.

Hockey is huge in Canada. The nation is captivated by the sport's combination of grace and brute force. Canadian children play all sorts of sports—baseball, football, basketball, and many more. But a lot of them *live* hockey. It's more than just a sport. It's a lifestyle. And that was never more true than in the case of Wayne Gretzky.

Walter had always been an avid hockey fan. He'd even played some minor league hockey in his youth. He wanted to be sure his son shared his love of the game.

HOCKEY TERMS

center: the front-line player who typically plays in the
center of the ice and takes most of the face-offs

face-off: the start of any sequence of play. The referee
drops the puck between a player from each team.

period: a twenty-minute segment of a hockey game.
Games have three periods.

power play: when one team has more players on the ice
than the other team due to a penalty

short-handed: playing with one or more players off the ice
in the penalty box

wingers: the front-line players who typically play on either
side of the center

zone: the area on each end of the ice, separated from
center ice by a blue line

Wayne took to the game right away. Almost as soon as he could walk, he was sliding around the Gretzkys' floor in his socks, pretending to skate. Walter had Wayne in a real pair of ice skates by age two. He got the little boy a regular-size hockey stick, cut down to Wayne's height, and sent him onto the ice of the nearby Nith River. Little Wayne wasted no time. From the start, he was a natural on skates. There was nothing he'd rather be doing.

"I was fortunate to have my dad as my first teacher," Wayne said. "He made the game simple and he made the game fun. He taught me the importance of a lot of hard work."

Wayne's life revolved around hockey. He watched it with his family on television. And he spent every spare minute on the neighborhood ice rinks. His parents did everything they could to encourage their son. But before long, Walter was tired of spending hours freezing in the car while Wayne was skating and shooting on the ice. Walter's solution was simple. He built a rink in the family's backyard. The days of driving Wayne from rink to rink were over. Walter could watch his talented young son without ever leaving the warmth of his home.

Meanwhile, the Gretzky family was growing. A daughter, Kim, came along two years after Wayne was born. Three brothers would follow—Keith, Glen, and Brent. But even with all of the additions, Walter and Phyllis always made time for Wayne.

By age five, Wayne was tired of just practicing. He wanted to join a real team. But despite his obvious skills, none of the area's youth leagues would take on a five-year-old. He had to wait until he was six before he could join the Brantford Atoms, a ten-and-under youth hockey team. Even when he did finally join the team in 1967, he was so small that he could barely fit into a uniform. His jersey hung so far down that he often got his stick caught in it. He learned to tuck one side into his pants—a style that he would maintain throughout his career.

That first year with the Atoms was tough. Wayne scored just one goal all year. He was in tears when he didn't win any awards at the end of the season. But his parents told him to keep working, so that's what he did.

 The Gretzky family called the rink in their backyard the Wally Coliseum, in honor of Walter.

The next season, Wayne showed remarkable improvement. He was still very undersized, but he was somehow able to keep up with the older boys. He scored twenty-seven goals for the Atoms. People wondered how such a little boy could be doing that well against ten-year-olds.

By age eight, Wayne really had people talking. Still one of the youngest boys in the league, he scored an amazing 104 goals in 1969–1970. His smooth, clean skating, accurate shots, and sharp reflexes seemed extraordinary for a child. His greatest asset, however, may have been his anticipation. He seemed to know ahead of time where the puck was headed. He was always a step or two ahead of the other boys.

As a nine-year-old, Wayne was virtually unstoppable. He blew the league away with 196 goals. His domination was earning him national attention. The media did stories on Brantford's hockey "prodigy." His talent seemed almost superhuman. Onlookers could only wonder what he might accomplish as a ten-year-old.

As he entered his final season for the Atoms, ten-year-old Wayne experienced intense pressure. All eyes were on the 4-foot-4 (1.3-meter) center. (Even though he was one of the older boys in the league, he was still short for his age.) Reporters wanted to interview him. Fans were asking him for autographs. He was on TV, had dozens of newspaper articles written about him, and brought huge crowds to Brantford's games. He also earned the nickname that would follow him throughout his career, the "Great Gretzky."

It was a terrible amount of pressure for a child. The attention was exhausting. Wayne sometimes switched jerseys with a teammate just so people would leave him alone for a while. He was shy and uncomfortable being the constant center of attention.

Still, that 1971–1972 season became the stuff of legend. Wayne was more dominant than ever. He scored 378 goals—almost three times the total of the next highest scorer. In addition, he had 120 assists. Together, his goals and assists added up to 498 points. (One of the most important statistics for a hockey player is points. This number is the sum of a player's goals and assists.) He'd smashed every youth scoring record imaginable.

As great as Wayne had played, he later remembered the season as the point at which hockey became more than just a game. "Hockey was no longer just fun," he wrote in his autobiography. "It became fun mixed with doses of fame and jealousy and ugliness."

❝ *It's only human nature that people would resent [Wayne] for scoring two hundred or three hundred goals in a season. If your boy is on the team, you're not going to be happy.* **❞**

—WALTER GRETZKY

Some players' parents were jealous of Wayne. They sometimes booed the young star. They accused him of hogging the puck. Wayne's high assist total, however, proved that he wasn't a selfish player. He was popular with his teammates and was a good team player. But that didn't stop people from booing him and shouting at him. Worse still, the abuse carried over to the other sports Wayne played. He wasn't as big a star in basketball, lacrosse, or baseball. But some parents still gave him a hard time. Once at a baseball game, an opposing coach told him, "You won't live to see Christmas, Gretzky."

Despite the difficulties, Wayne continued to excel on Brantford's youth teams. In 1974, at age thirteen, he led his team to the Quebec International Pee Wee Hockey Tournament. There, they played the top youth hockey teams from around North America. The games were held at the Colisee, home of the World Hockey Association's (WHA) Quebec Nordiques. In his first game, Wayne scored seven goals and added four assists. That achievement tied the tournament's single-game scoring record set by Guy Lafleur, who went on to play in the NHL. With his record-setting performance, Wayne's fame only grew. And with it grew the jealousy of some other parents.

GORDIE HOWE

If Wayne idolized one player, it was Gordie Howe. Howe, born in 1928, was one of the game's all-time greats. In a 1971 newspaper interview, Wayne said, "Gordie Howe is my kind of player. He had so many tricks around the net, no wonder he scored so many goals. I'd like to be just like him."

After Wayne's team was knocked out of the tournament in the semifinals, the team returned home. The abuse in Brantford continued. Soon, Wayne didn't even feel welcome in his own hometown. It was time for a change.

Chapter | Two

A New Start

Wayne was deeply hurt by all the criticism. He was miserable at home. So in 1975, when he got an offer to play for a junior team in nearby Toronto (about sixty miles from Brantford), he jumped at the chance. He convinced his parents to let him go, packed his bags, and headed to a new team and a new school in Toronto. He'd live with the family of another player during the week and return home on the weekends. Wayne would be out of Brantford with a fresh start. He hoped in Toronto he could be just another player.

"A lot of people thought I moved away from home to be a hockey player, but that's not why," he later said. "I moved away just to try to escape all the pressures that [people] place on kids."

Wayne had planned to join a team of boys his own age. But because of technicalities in league rules, he wasn't allowed to do so. Instead, he ended up on a higher-level team, the Peterborough Petes. The team was at the Junior B level of the Ontario Hockey Association (OHA). Wayne, fourteen years old and weighing just 135 pounds, would be playing with and against players as old as twenty. For almost any player, that would be a huge challenge. But not for Wayne. He scored two goals in his first game and led his team to a 4–2 win. The fourteen-year-old prodigy was every bit as good as advertised.

Wayne is a huge baseball fan. Growing up, he wanted to play for his favorite team, the Detroit Tigers.

Wayne's success continued. He scored twenty-seven goals and added thirty-three assists that season. His efforts earned him the league's Rookie of the Year award.

Life off the ice was very different for Wayne. He enjoyed not being the center of attention as he'd been in Brantford. He didn't even tell many of his school friends that he was a hockey player. When one of them found out, Wayne begged him to keep it a secret. He couldn't bear the thought of being singled out again. He just wanted to be one of the guys.

In 1976 Wayne led his new team, the Toronto Nationals, to the playoffs. His regular season—thirty-six goals and thirty-six assists—had been great, but he really excelled in the playoffs. Over twenty-three playoff games, he tallied an amazing seventy-five points and led the team to the league championship. His success caught the attention of a lot of people. Scouts for professional teams in the WHA and NHL were starting to look closely at the fifteen-year-old center.

The next step was Major Junior A hockey, a sort of professional minor league. In 1977 Wayne was eligible for the league's draft. It was a nervous time for the Gretzky family. They had no control over who drafted Wayne. Walter wrote several of the most distant teams, begging them not to select his son. But the letters did no good. The Sault Sainte Marie Greyhounds took Wayne with the third pick in the draft. If he wanted to advance his career, he had to move five hundred miles from Brantford.

The Gretzkys flew to meet team owner Angelo Bumbacco. They intended to tell him that Wayne wouldn't play so far from home. But on the trip, Wayne was so impressed with Bumbacco, the town, and his teammates that he changed his mind. He joined the team at a salary of $25 per week plus expenses. That was plenty for a kid still in high school. (He went to school during the day and spent the rest of the time playing and practicing.)

Wayne's confidence never waned. He told his coach before the season that he'd be the league's leading scorer. It was an uncharacteristic boast for the usually shy Wayne, but he intended to back it up.

NINETY-NINE

When Wayne joined the Greyhounds, he wanted to wear number 9 (Howe's number). He was disappointed to learn that another player already had that number.

Wayne tried a few different numbers, including 19. One day, his coach suggested wearing number 99. It was unusual for a player to wear a number that high, and the number has since become associated with Wayne. In fact, in poker, many players refer to a starting hand of two nines as the Gretzky.

In his first game, Wayne made a big impression. He scored three goals and added three assists in leading his team to victory over the Oshawa Generals. His excellent play continued throughout the season, but he wasn't able to make good on his boast. Even though he broke the league's old scoring record with 182 points, Bobby Smith also broke the record, scoring 192.

After that season, Wayne felt like he was ready for the big time. Because he was just seventeen, he couldn't play in the NHL, which required players to be at least twenty. So he turned to the WHA, a league that started in 1971 to compete with the more popular NHL.

Before he took the ice for the WHA, though, Wayne had one thing to do. He'd been selected to represent his country at the 1978 World Junior Hockey Tournament in Quebec. He led the Canadian team to the bronze medal, scoring seventeen points in the tournament.

❝ *People talk about skating, puck handling, and shooting, but the whole sport is angles and [bounces], forgetting the straight direction the puck is going, calculating where it will be diverted, factoring in all interruptions. Basically, my whole game is angles.* ❞

—WAYNE GRETZKY

With that, Wayne was set for the pros. Wayne, his father, and his agent (a family friend named Gus Badali) weighed several offers from WHA teams. They finally agreed to sign with the Indianapolis Racers. Wayne's four-year contract totaled $825,000. It was more money than a seventeen-year-old kid knew how to spend. With so much money coming in and his hockey career taking off, Wayne dropped out of high school. He was one class short of graduating.

Wayne arrived in Indianapolis, Indiana, with a lot of pressure. A merge between the NHL and the WHA was widely rumored. But only a few of the most successful WHA teams would actually be absorbed into the NHL. The Racers weren't a good team. They lost more games than they won and often played before a lot of empty seats. Owner Nelson Skalbania was taking a big chance that the 155-pound Wayne could elevate the franchise. But the move was also a risk for Wayne. If the leagues merged, the NHL might not allow him to play because of his age.

> Early in Wayne's career, he suffered from an intense fear of flying in airplanes. He knew he had to overcome the fear because professional athletes spend a lot of time on planes, flying from game to game. He went to a hypnotist to help him deal with the fear.

Wayne's professional debut was forgettable. As famous as Wayne had become in Canada, few people in Indianapolis had ever heard of him. Crowds didn't flock to the gates as Skalbania had hoped. And Wayne himself did little to generate excitement, scoring just three goals and three assists in eight games. Soon the team was losing too much money to stay in business. Skalbania told Wayne that he had to trade him. He gave the young center a choice—Edmonton or Winnipeg.

Wayne didn't need to think very long. He wanted to join the Edmonton Oilers in Alberta, Canada. It was a strong, popular franchise. If the WHA and NHL merged, Edmonton would be first on the list to become an NHL team.

All the moving around was a lot to take. On his eighteenth birthday, Wayne signed a ten-year contract with the Oilers. It contained options that could keep Wayne under contract until 1999—twenty-one years in total. Even though the contract was so long, everyone understood that it would have to be reworked within a year or two. The strange way the contract was set up was largely to get the NHL's attention.

While Wayne's life off the ice was hectic, he remained confident on the ice. He finished third in the WHA with 110 points and forty-six goals. Those numbers earned him the league's 1979 Rookie of the Year award. One highlight of the season was his selection to the WHA All-Star Team. The WHA All-Stars played a three-game series against a team of stars from the Soviet Union (a group of republics including Russia). The WHA players won all three games. Wayne got to be on a line with his childhood idol, Gordie Howe.

The Oilers were winning as well. They finished in first place in the six-team league but lost the championship to the Winnipeg Jets, four games to two. It would prove to be the WHA's final series. After the season, the long-awaited merger finally happened. Four of the league's six teams, including Edmonton, became NHL franchises. Better yet, the NHL agreed not to enforce its age restriction for WHA players under twenty years of age. Number 99 was coming to the world's best hockey league.

Chapter | Three

Building a Dynasty

Joining a bigger, better league would be a big challenge for Wayne and the Oilers. The fans in Edmonton were excited. Ticket sales soared. But most experts expected the four new teams to struggle. And nobody knew what to expect from Wayne. His small size could be a major drawback with the NHL's physical style of play. Could he withstand the punishment? Could he handle the pressure of playing against the best players in the world?

"I've had pressure all along," Wayne said. "There's always going to be pressure on a professional athlete. I can't think about it."

Things started out rough. The Oilers were losing, and Wayne didn't have a goal until the team's fifth game. Even that goal was a weak dribbler that went into the net almost by accident. Making things worse, Wayne's throat was hurting him. He had a bad case of tonsillitis (an infection of the tonsils). At one point in the season, he was so sick that he lost 11 pounds. That was weight the already skinny center couldn't afford to lose.

But in time, Wayne's scoring picked up, and the Oilers became more competitive. Soon the NHL was seeing why Wayne Gretzky was such a big name. He began running up big totals for goals and assists, just as he had at every level of hockey he'd ever played. At midseason, he was named to the All-Star team.

In the second half of the season, his play continued to push him up the scoring charts. A game against the powerful Montreal Canadiens gave Wayne a chance to show his dominance. The underdog Oilers dominated Montreal. In the 9–1 win, Wayne tallied seven points—one shy of the NHL single-game record.

On April 2, 1980, the nineteen-year-old center scored his fiftieth goal. He was the youngest player in NHL history to do so. By season's end, his 137 points tied Marcel Dionne of the Los Angeles Kings for the most in the league. Because Dionne had more goals than Wayne, he won the Art Ross Trophy as the league's scoring champion. Wayne was disappointed that he didn't win the scoring title, but he got an even better surprise after the season. He was awarded the Hart Memorial Trophy as the league's MVP. He also won the league's sportsmanship award for the way he conducted himself on and off the ice.

After that kind of a season, nobody had doubts anymore. Wayne Gretzky belonged in the NHL. More than anything, teammates and opponents marveled at how well he could anticipate where the puck was going to be. "Gretzky sees a picture out there that no one else sees," said Boston Bruins president Harry Sinden. "It's difficult to describe because I've never seen the game he's looking at."

Wayne wasn't just having personal success. The team was also doing well. The Oilers went on a remarkable winning streak to end the season. The late surge pushed Edmonton to a 28-39-13 record and into the league's final playoff spot. Against all odds, the first-year team was headed to the postseason.

Edmonton's dream season came to an abrupt but expected end in the playoffs. As the sixteen seed (the worst of all sixteen playoff teams), they had to play the Philadelphia Flyers, who had earned the number one seed by having the league's best record. It was a best-of-five series, meaning the first team to win three games would advance to the second round. The Flyers were more talented and more experienced, and they swept the Oilers in three games (although two of the three games went into overtime). Despite the loss, the 1979–1980 season had been a tremendous success. The former WHA team held up well in the new league. And the Oilers' young, undersized center showed that he would be an NHL force for years to come.

The success carried over in 1980–1981. The Oilers were a team on the rise. Future stars Paul Coffey and Jari Kurri joined the team before the season. Together with Wayne, Mark Messier, and the team's core of young talent, they helped Edmonton get out to a hot start.

JARI KURRI

Jari Kurri, born in Finland in 1960, was one of Wayne's most notable teammates. Kurri began his career in a Finnish league before joining the Edmonton Oilers. The "Finnish Flash" enjoyed his best season in 1984–1985, when he scored 135 points. The next year, he led the NHL in goals with sixty-eight.

In addition to Edmonton, Kurri also played for the Los Angeles Kings, the New York Rangers, the Anaheim Mighty Ducks, and the Colorado Avalanche. He was elected to the Hockey Hall of Fame in 2001.

Wayne, still just nineteen years old, was dominant. The league had never seen anything like him. He had an unparalleled feel for the game. Physically, he was small. The league had faster skaters, better puck handlers, and players with more powerful shots. But nobody could match Wayne's all-around instincts. He always seemed to be in the right place at the right time. By March, he was chasing down Phil Esposito's single-season scoring record of 152 points. It was almost unthinkable that a second-year player who had just turned twenty could break one of the NHL's greatest records.

On March 29, Wayne skated onto the ice in Pittsburgh tied with Esposito at 152 points. Even though he was in the Penguins' stadium, the fans were eager to see the record broken. Wayne didn't make them wait long. In the first period, with the Oilers on a power play, he took the puck into the Pittsburgh zone. He skated around a defender and took the puck behind the net— one of his favorite places to survey the ice. As he watched, he saw Messier break free of his defender out in front of the goal. He wasted no time in flicking a quick pass to his teammate. Messier slapped the puck cleanly into the net for the goal. The assist gave Wayne his 153rd point of the season and sole possession of the record. The Pittsburgh fans gave him a standing ovation. They knew that they'd witnessed a special moment. Wayne added two more assists in the game, a 5–2 victory.

That was just one of many magical nights for Wayne in 1980–1981. By season's end, he had a record 109 assists and 55 goals. He won the Art Ross Trophy for the scoring title as well as the Hart Trophy as the MVP. More important, he helped Edmonton earn a playoff spot.

Despite Wayne's brilliance, few expected the young Oilers to compete with the powerful Montreal Canadiens in the series. Montreal was an experienced team that had won several Stanley Cups (NHL titles). The Canadiens were playoff-tested, rarely lost at home, and were heavy favorites to dispose of the Oilers. Still, as Wayne and his teammates stepped onto the ice for game one in Montreal, they felt strangely confident. As their coach, Glen Sather, had told them, they had nothing to lose. They were *supposed* to get beat.

If the Canadiens expected an easy series, Wayne quickly changed those ideas. He got a playoff-record five assists in leading the Oilers to a surprising 6–3 victory. One loss stunned Montreal. But the second one was a complete shock. Wayne and the Oilers followed up the win with a 3–1 victory in game two.

Montreal barely had time to react. The underdog had a 2–0 lead and was one game away from advancing. Worse still for the Canadiens, the next two games were scheduled to take place on the Oilers' home ice in Edmonton.

Wayne knew what a huge opportunity this was, and he wasn't about to let it slip away. He didn't want to give Montreal any hope of a comeback. In game three, Wayne dominated the ice, scoring a hat trick and adding an assist in an easy 6–2 win. As the final buzzer sounded, he and his teammates celebrated one of the biggest playoff upsets in NHL history. An elated Wayne asked a reporter, "Do you think anyone in the NHL believes this?"

The celebration was short-lived, however. Edmonton's reward for advancing was a series against the defending Stanley Cup champions, the New York Islanders. The Oilers entered the second-round series with a similar nothing-to-lose outlook. New York was a better, more experienced team, and Edmonton wasn't supposed to be able to keep up.

HAT TRICK

In hockey, the term *hat trick* was first used in Toronto in the 1940s. A Toronto retailer would give a free hat to any Toronto Maple Leaf player who scored three goals in a game. The term's origin may go back to the English game of cricket, where teams used to reward players with hats for good performances.

It was a physical, hard-fought series. The Oilers gave the Islanders all they could handle. But the second round was a best-of-seven series, unlike the shorter five-game series in the first round. Longer series favor the stronger, tougher teams, and that held true in the 4–2 Islander series victory. Edmonton's season was over. But its players and fans had every reason to be excited about their team. Nobody would be taking this former WHA franchise lightly again.

1981 CANADA CUP

In the summer of 1981, Wayne was selected to represent his country in an international tournament called the Canada Cup. Canada was a heavy favorite to win the tournament. They quickly showed why, beating Finland 9–0 and the United States 8–3. Wayne was racking up goals and assists, and Canada looked unstoppable. But in the championship game, the Soviet Union handed Canada a shocking defeat, 8–1. It was one of the most embarrassing losses of Wayne's career.

After setting an assists record in 1980–1981, Wayne was determined to score more goals in 1981–1982. He was already the NHL's most dangerous scorer, but he knew he could do more.

His determination paid off. Early in the season, he was scoring goals at an unheard-of pace, making opposing defenders and goaltenders look almost silly. By the time he scored his fiftieth goal in his thirty-ninth game, his season was already legendary. But Wayne didn't stop there. He kept on scoring. Soon, he was chasing down Esposito's record of seventy-six goals in a single season. As Wayne got close to the record, Esposito began following the team around so he could be on hand for the record breaker.

Wayne actually worried about making Esposito wait. He didn't want to make one of his childhood heroes fly all around the United States and Canada just on his account. So he stepped up his pace. On February 24, 1982, the Oilers were playing in Buffalo, New York. In the third period, Wayne stole the puck, made a move, and rifled a one-timer (single hard shot) past the Buffalo goalie. He'd done it—seventy-seven goals, with more than a month yet to play! Esposito came onto the ice to congratulate Wayne, then the game resumed. For good measure, Wayne added two more goals before the final buzzer sounded. "My biggest thought," Wayne later said, "was 'Oh good, Phil [Esposito] can go home.'"

The Oilers kept winning, and Wayne kept scoring. He finished with an amazing 92 goals and 120 assists and became the first player to score 200 points or more in a season. Considering that just a year before, the NHL record had been 152, the feat simply had no parallel. The league's MVP wasn't just breaking records—he was destroying them. Despite being only twenty-one years old, Wayne had already convinced most fans and experts that he was the greatest hockey player the world had ever known.

YOUNG AND RESTLESS

By the early 1980s, Wayne was becoming a household name in the United States as well as in Canada. His newfound celebrity status gave him the chance to make some television appearances. He had a small guest role on a soap opera called *The Young and the Restless*. He also served as a judge on the TV dance contest *Dance Fever*.

Wayne's heroics led the Oilers to the second-best record in the NHL, 48-17-15. Their first-round playoff opponent was the Los Angeles Kings. Just as Montreal had been a heavy favorite over Edmonton the year before, the Oilers were expected to handle the weaker Kings without any problems. But like the Canadiens, Wayne and his teammates discovered that being the favorite doesn't guarantee anything. The Oilers seemed sluggish on the ice. The underdog Kings quickly built a 2–1 series lead and were a win away from advancing.

In game four, the Oilers gave it everything they had and held on for a slim 3–2 victory. That forced a deciding game five, held in Edmonton. With momentum on their side and the game on their home ice, the Oilers were confident. They were the better team, and they intended to show it.

It didn't work out that way, though. The Kings played energetic and inspired hockey, while Edmonton looked like a tired team. As the clock ticked down to zero, the Oilers hung their heads in defeat. The score was 7–4. A year before, they'd been the upstarts. Now they knew what it felt like to be on the other end of an upset. Wayne's historic regular season had ended with a bitter postseason disappointment.

Chapter | Four

Cup Dreams

Wayne and his teammates knew that personal milestones meant little when the team failed to make it past the first round of the playoffs. For this reason, Coach Sather decided that Wayne would spend less time on the ice during the 1982–1983 regular season. After averaging about twenty-six minutes per game in the previous season, Wayne had been exhausted during the playoffs. By reducing Wayne's ice time during the regular season, Sather hoped he'd be fresher for the postseason.

As expected, Wayne's numbers went down a little. He scored seventy-one goals and had 125 assists. His 196 total points were a dropoff from 1981–1982, but it still ranked as one of the greatest seasons in NHL history. For the fourth straight year, Wayne was the league's MVP. No one before had ever won four Hart Trophies in a row.

Wayne started out the 1982–1983 season by scoring in each of Edmonton's first thirty games, breaking the old record of twenty-eight.

Once again, Edmonton won its division and was a heavy first-round playoffs favorite. This time, they didn't take their opponent—the Winnipeg Jets—lightly. Number 99 was fresh and ready for action. Although the games were close, Edmonton swept the Jets in three games. It was a big step toward forgetting their 1982 embarrassment against the Kings.

Next up were the Calgary Flames, one of Edmonton's biggest rivals. Wayne, Messier, and Kurri teamed up to completely dominate the Flames. The highlight of the series for Wayne came in game three. After opening the scoring on an assist to Coffey, Wayne started looking for his own shot. His first goal came off the stick of Glenn Anderson, who found Wayne down the ice for a breakaway goal. Next, Wayne blasted a pass from Kurri for goal number two. A tip near the net gave him a hat trick. But he wasn't done yet. On a backhanded flick near the net, he tied a playoff record for goals. Finally, he added two more assists—four goals and three assists in a single game! The seven points was an NHL playoff record and left no doubt as to which was the dominant team. The Oilers took the series four games to one.

In the conference finals, the Oilers met the Chicago Blackhawks. Chicago was a good team, but its players seemed completely overmatched by Edmonton. After blowing out the Blackhawks in the first two games, the Oilers cruised to a four-game sweep. They were headed to the Stanley Cup finals!

The team had never been more confident. People sometimes forgot that Edmonton was one of the NHL's younger teams. Gretzky had already been in the league for four years, but he was still just twenty-two years old. Most players don't even enter their prime playing years until their mid- to late twenties.

A Good Sport (with Bad Timing)

In 1982 *Sports Illustrated* named Wayne "Sportsman of the Year." It was a huge honor for the young center because the magazine was recognizing his excellent sportsmanship as well as his skills.

That year Wayne had been speaking out against the common practice of fighting in the NHL. But the night *Sports Illustrated* was presenting the award to Wayne, he got into a fight with Minnesota's Neal Broten. Wayne participated in only a handful of real fights in his career. This one had the worst possible timing.

Their finals opponent, the Islanders, didn't lack confidence either. They'd won three Stanley Cups in recent years and were the more experienced team. That experience showed early. New York took game one, 2–0. In game two, things got ugly. New York goalie Billy Smith slashed Wayne hard across the leg with his stick. Wayne fell to the ice. Furious, he got up to confront the goalie. The two men were set for a fight—a true rarity (Wayne almost never fought, and goaltenders rarely take part in fights). But officials quickly stepped in and broke them up.

For Edmonton, the damage was done. Wayne's leg hurt so badly that he ended up having to leave the ice. Whether Smith's slash was a tactic to intimidate the young Oilers or an accident (as he insisted it was), only he knows. But the incident rattled Edmonton, and they lost the game 6–3. Trailing the series 2–0, their Stanley Cup hopes were looking dim.

Edmonton fans hoped the controversy would spark their team. But Smith was red hot, and the Oilers just couldn't keep up with the high-scoring Islanders. New York won games three and four for a series sweep. Despite having the league's best regular-season record, the Oilers had again come up empty in the post-season. For Wayne, who was shut out in the series, the criticism was especially loud. Critics said that he wasn't suited for the physical style of the playoffs. Until he could bring his team a title, his amazing statistics and records didn't mean much.

After the series, Wayne apologized to his teammates and fans. "My job is to put the puck in the net," he said. "I just didn't."

As the 1983–1984 season approached, the team knew it needed to make some changes. One big change came when Wayne took over as team captain—the leader of the team both on and off the ice. Lee Fogolin, the previous captain, knew that the Oilers were built around Wayne. He wanted to give Wayne the lead in spirit as well as in name. For Wayne, the C added to his jersey was an honor and a responsibility. More than ever, Edmonton was *Wayne's* team.

That wasn't the only change, though. The 1983 Stanley Cup finals had shown Wayne and the Oilers the importance of being tough. Wayne worked out hard during the off-season, adding ten pounds of muscle to his lean frame.

The difference showed. Wayne was stronger than ever. To start the season, he broke his own record of scoring in each of the team's first thirty games. As the season continued, the record just kept growing. Soon, the scoring streak had climbed to forty games. One of the highlights of the streak was the forty-first game, in which Wayne had four goals and four assists against the Minnesota North Stars.

To the casual observer, Wayne looked better than ever. But a big problem was developing. Wayne's shoulder ached badly from a hit he'd taken earlier in the season. With an NHL record on the line every night, however, he didn't dare take the rest he badly needed. He had to stay on the ice to keep the streak alive.

During his amazing scoring streak to start the 1983–1984 season, Wayne got superstitious. So one game when he couldn't find his lucky garter belt (equipment to hold up his socks), he panicked. He tore up a new garter belt to look worn like his old one. He scored four points that night, so it must have worked!

In the forty-fourth game, the streak almost ended against the Blackhawks. But in the final minute, with Edmonton ahead 4–3, Chicago pulled its goalie for an extra attacker. With just seven seconds left, Wayne stole the puck at center ice. He charged toward the other end and flicked it into the empty net with just one second remaining. The streak lived on.

Soon, the streak passed fifty games. Fans started to wonder if Wayne could do something that seemed impossible—score a point in every game of the eighty-game season. But Wayne knew better. His shoulder was getting worse. After some games, he could barely move it. The streak finally ended in the fifty-second game against the Kings. Wayne was almost relieved because he could finally rest his shoulder. He didn't play a single minute in Edmonton's next six games.

"This may have been one of the harder records to break," Wayne said of the streak. "When you score ninety goals or break the record for points, you can do that over eighty games. But the streak itself is pressure every night to be at your best, be consistent game-in and game-out."

For Wayne and his teammates, the regular season was just a long warm-up for the playoffs. The team had a potent offense, setting an NHL record with 446 goals. Wayne again won the scoring title with 205 points, including eighty-seven goals. To the surprise of no one, he earned another Hart Trophy. The Oilers, meanwhile, were the most feared team in the league. They were ready for the playoffs. Anything less than a Stanley Cup would be a failure.

The playoffs started with a sweep of Winnipeg. In the second round, the Flames gave Edmonton all they could handle, but Wayne and his teammates held on for a 4–3 series win.

Their opponent for the conference finals was the North Stars. Minnesota, hit hard by injuries, stood no chance. Even when the North Stars had a three-goal lead in game three, the Oilers stormed back, scoring the game's next six goals. Edmonton swept the series to advance to the Stanley Cup finals, where they would once again face the Islanders. This time, they didn't intend to come up short.

In 1983 Wayne got himself into a rare bit of controversy when he called the New Jersey Devils a "Mickey Mouse operation." Devils fans held a grudge against Wayne for years. They'd bring signs to the game that read *Gretzky is Goofy*.

The series opened in New York. It was a defensive struggle. Goalies Grant Fuhr and Billy Smith were strong in the net, and the game's only goal came from Oiler center Kevin McClelland. It wasn't a typical Oiler victory, and Wayne was concerned about the team's ability to get the puck past Smith. But a win was a win.

The good feelings disappeared in game two when New York crushed the Oilers 6–1. The blowout forced Edmonton to question how they were going to beat Smith. In six Stanley Cup finals games over the past two years, Wayne had yet to score a goal. Once again, the criticisms of his toughness surfaced.

Fortunately the Oilers pulled off another win in game three. Although Wayne still hadn't scored a goal, the Oilers were up 2–1.

Wayne's scoring drought was no accident. The Islanders knew who the most dangerous player on the ice was. Their defenders stuck to Wayne like glue. Even when he didn't have the puck, they always kept a man on him. But in game four, Wayne made an adjustment to his passing. He started waiting longer to pass the puck, fighting through checks (collisions with other players) before he let it go. The change threw off the Islanders' defense, and Wayne finally slapped one past Smith. Wayne later admitted that he felt a huge weight lift off his shoulders once he scored that first goal. He felt even better later in the game when he added a second goal and helped the Oilers to another blowout victory. With a 3–1 series lead, they needed just one more win to claim the championship.

Before game five, Wayne stood up in front of his teammates. He'd always been quiet and wasn't one to make speeches. But this time, he had something to say. "I've won a lot of awards in my life," he said. "I've had a lot of personal success. But nothing I've ever done means more than this."

After a scoreless first period, Wayne took over. Twice, Kurri found him with a perfect pass, and Wayne drove both of them past Smith. By the start of the third period, the Oilers led 3–0, and the Islanders had replaced Smith as goalie. Edmonton was twenty minutes away from the title. The Islanders didn't make it easy, though. They scored twice in the period. But that was all. When the final buzzer sounded, Edmonton had a 5–2 victory. The team stormed onto the ice to celebrate the Oilers' first Stanley Cup championship.

As soon as the Stanley Cup came onto the ice, Wayne skated over and grabbed it. He and his teammates held up the trophy as the Canadian fans went crazy. Wayne was as happy as he'd ever been on the ice.

"To be a champion changes everything, just the way you feel about coming to the rink," Wayne later said. "Many a time I've stared and stared at the Stanley Cup."

Winning the Cup was like a dream, and Wayne couldn't wait to defend the title. But before the 1984–1985 season, he helped the Canadian national team reclaim the Canada Cup. The Soviet Union lost in the semifinals, so Canada faced Sweden in the finals. Winning the tournament was a great feeling after the team's failure in 1981.

Wayne's real focus was on repeating as Stanley Cup champs, however. As the season approached in the fall of

1984, the media's demands on the twenty-three-year-old center were higher than ever. Companies wanted him to endorse their products. Reporters constantly wanted interviews with hockey's greatest player. Wayne was so famous that he could barely go out in public without being mobbed by fans and autograph seekers. He took it all in stride, though. He was used to attention. He'd been in the public eye for almost two decades.

Despite the championship, some critics still questioned the Oilers. The team had a reputation as not being very tough physically. The team was built around offense rather than defense, an imbalance that some people saw as a weakness. Many NHL experts believed that championship-caliber teams had to stress defense. They thought Edmonton's victory in 1984 might have been a fluke.

The Oilers started proving the critics wrong. They were unbeaten in their first fifteen games. In December, Wayne reached a big personal milestone with his 1,000th career point. This feat had taken him just five and a half seasons, by far the fastest in NHL history. Better still, the Oilers kept winning. The team finished the season with a record of 49-20-11. Wayne broke his own assists record with 135. With his seventy-three goals, he again eclipsed 200 points in a season and was the league's MVP.

But the regular season had become almost a formality for the Oilers. Wayne and his teammates just wanted the Stanley Cup again. "The Cup is addictive," Wayne wrote in his autobiography. "You think it's yours, and so you become like a selfish kid—you don't want anybody else to touch it, see it, have it, or study it."

The Oilers opened the playoffs by sweeping the Kings. Even though the series ended 3–0, it wasn't easy. Two of the three games went into overtime. The Winnipeg Jets were up next. The Oilers won the first three games, and Wayne made it a sweep by scoring three goals and adding four assists in game four.

The conference finals, again against the Blackhawks, were a back-and-forth battle. The Oilers dominated the first two games in Edmonton, pushing their playoff winning streak to nine games. But when the series moved to Chicago, the Blackhawks came to life and tied the series 2–2. It was a minor scare for the Oilers, who had been cruising along. But once the series returned to Edmonton, they took over. Blowout victories in games five and six sent them once again to the Stanley Cup finals.

There, a new opponent waited—the Philadelphia Flyers. The Flyers had the league's best regular-season record. They played a tough, physical style, and they focused on slowing down number 99. Wayne even suspected the Flyers of making their ice choppy to slow down the Oilers, who relied on speed. In game one, Philadelphia's strategy worked perfectly. They held Wayne scoreless and skated to a 4–1 win. A newspaper article the next day called the Oilers a fraud.

Edmonton didn't need any extra motivation, but the article got their attention. In another defensive struggle, they evened the series at 1–1. They carried that momentum back to Edmonton with back-to-back wins in tight games. Game three provided one of Wayne's series highlights. He scored two goals in the game's first two minutes and a total of three in the first period. He added a fourth goal later, as well as two assists. Then in game four, he led the Oilers back from a two-goal deficit. The comeback win gave the team a 3–1 series lead.

Game five was the last game scheduled to be played in Edmonton. Wayne and his teammates badly wanted to win the title in front of their home fans. They came out strong, with one of Wayne's best plays of the year. Coffey flicked Wayne a pass into the Flyer zone, then sped down the ice to catch up to the play. Wayne took the puck, then quickly returned it, behind his back, to Coffey. Coffey never broke his stride as he fired it past the Flyer goaltender.

That great play was just the start of an amazing night in Edmonton. The Oilers tallied seven goals in the first two periods and cruised to a series-clinching 8–3 victory. Wayne and his Oilers were no fluke. They were the two-time Stanley Cup champs. They'd gone an amazing 15–4 in the playoffs, and Wayne had scored a career-high forty-seven postseason points. His performance earned him the playoff MVP award.

There was no longer any doubt—the Oilers were for real. They were the NHL's best team, and twenty-four-year-old Wayne Gretzky was already the greatest player the game had ever seen. Wayne didn't face any more questions about whether he was big enough or tough enough. The only question was how long Edmonton's dynasty would last.

Chapter | Five

The Mighty Oilers

At first glance, 1985–1986 might have looked like a down season for Wayne. He scored "just" fifty-two goals, by far his lowest total in five years. But while his goals were down, his assists skyrocketed. He destroyed his own assists record with 163—averaging more than two assists per game. He also broke his own points record with 215, a record many experts think of as unbreakable. Wayne's goals might have been down, but the season was still one of the best of his career. To nobody's surprise, he won his seventh straight Hart Trophy as the league MVP.

Meanwhile, the Oilers enjoyed one of their finest regular seasons at 56-17-7. Heading into the playoffs with the league's best record, they looked unstoppable. Their dominance carried into the first round of the playoffs, a 3–0 sweep of the Vancouver Canucks. In the series, Edmonton outscored Vancouver 17–5.

After having such an easy time in the first round, the two-time defending champs were supremely confident. They entered the second-round series against the Calgary Flames feeling unbeatable. But before long, the Oilers realized that they were in for a fight. The Flames won game one, 4–1. In game two, Edmonton needed overtime to salvage a 1–1 series tie.

It was a hard-fought series. Calgary gave Wayne a lot of defensive attention. The strategy worked, and they skated to a 3–2 series lead. The Oilers had to win both games six and seven or their hopes of winning three straight Cups would be over.

The Oilers did their part in game six, winning 5–2. That set up a deciding game seven, played in Edmonton. Despite having the home ice, things started to go wrong for the Oilers early in the game, and they fell behind 2–0. The mood of the fans and players was nervous, even after Edmonton scored to reduce the deficit to one goal.

Late in the second period, Edmonton tied the game at two, and the confidence began to return. Wayne and his teammates felt that it was only a matter of time before they took the lead. But then disaster struck. Late in the game, Edmonton defense-man Steve Smith tried to clear (pass) the puck from behind the Oilers' net. The puck hit Fuhr on the back of the leg and bounced back into the goal. The Flames had just taken a 3–2 lead without even touching the puck. The Oilers never recovered from the mistake. The game ended 3–2, and Edmonton's season was shockingly over.

Reporters and fans were hard on Smith. But Wayne and the team refused to blame the young defenseman for the loss. His mistake had been one play in a seven-game series. "I gave them a plan and they didn't follow it," said coach Glen Sather.

The painful loss made the Oilers even more determined in 1986–1987. Sather signed star defenseman Reijo Ruotsalainen to a contract, adding more depth to the Oilers' already strong core of players. By the fall of 1986, the team was anxious to get started on their quest to reclaim the Stanley Cup.

As usual, Wayne led the league in scoring, but his streak of 200-point seasons came to an end. Still, nobody was complaining. Sixty-two goals and 121 assists might have been a down year for Wayne statistically, but he was still easily the league's MVP. That a 183-point output could be thought of as a down year showed how dominant number 99 had become.

Part of the reason for the decline in scoring was the team's new philosophy. The Oilers had always been known as an offensive force. But in 1986–1987, Sather wanted the team to commit to tougher defense. With the shift in attention, the Oiler offense dropped off a bit, though still remained strong. The new defensive mind-set, however, paid off. The Oilers posted the league's best record. Once again, they were prepared for a strong postseason run.

The playoffs opened with a minor scare—a 5–2 loss at home to the Kings. The NHL had switched the first-round format to seven games that year, however, so the Oilers had plenty of time to get back on their feet. They won the next four games to advance.

ABOVE THE FRAY

Many NHL fans noticed how infrequently Wayne took big hits from his opponents. Part of the reason for this was his great vision and anticipation. He could see the big checks coming and get out of the way. Another reason is that over the years, most of his teams had big, tough "enforcers," or bodyguards. Opponents knew that if they hit Wayne, bruisers like Dave Semenko or Marty McSorley would hit them back—twice as hard!

Four more wins against the Jets made it eight in a row. The Oilers' dominance continued in the conference finals with a 4–1 series win over Detroit. The Oilers were destroying every team they faced. They looked unbeatable.

"We took every single shift in those playoffs dead seriously," Wayne later wrote. "The last thing we were going to do . . . was be overconfident."

The 1987 Stanley Cup finals featured a dream matchup for hockey fans. The Oilers faced the league's second-best team, the Flyers, in a rematch of the 1985 Stanley Cup finals. Edmonton came out strong, winning the first two games at home.

Early in the series, Wayne became the center of a controversy. Flyer coach Mike Keenan accused him of "diving." He claimed that Wayne was falling down on purpose to make the officials believe he had been tripped. The Flyers claimed that they were getting called for penalties that Wayne had tricked the officials into calling.

"You expect more from the best player in the world," Keenan said. "All he's doing is embarrassing the officials."

Wayne denied diving, at least in this instance. He later admitted that he would sometimes dive to get a call but said that it was a common practice among players. And he insisted that it hadn't happened against the Flyers in the Stanley Cup finals.

After dropping game three, the Oilers won to take a commanding 3–1 series lead. Philly was more determined than ever to contain number 99 in game five in Edmonton. They did a good job and held on for a 4–3 victory. Game six in Philadelphia was a similar affair. The Flyers again won a physical, tightly contested game,

3–2. The win pulled them even with the Oilers at three games apiece. NHL fans were set to see something that hadn't happened in sixteen years—a game seven of the Stanley Cup finals.

The buildup for that final game—to be played in Edmonton—was enormous. For players and coaches, it was the ultimate test—one game, winner take all. Nobody needed any extra motivation. They all knew that this was the game they'd dreamed of all their lives.

Momentum was firmly on Philadelphia's side, a feeling that continued early in game seven. Back-to-back penalties left the Oilers trying to kill a five-on-three power play. Skating with a two-man disadvantage is a difficult task against any team, but against a team as good as the Flyers, it was an almost hopeless situation. Sure enough, the Flyers took advantage with the game's first goal.

Despite everything that had happened, Wayne and his teammates refused to get discouraged. Within minutes, the Oilers had tied the game. Shortly after that, Wayne spotted Kurri in front of the Flyer net. He slid a perfect pass to his teammate, and Kurri slapped it home—2–1 Oilers! From that moment, Edmonton focused on defense. They fell back and clamped down on Philly's scorers.

As the third-period clock ticked down, the building was buzzing. Then, with less than three minutes to go, the Oilers sealed the win with another goal. The fans erupted. On the ice, Edmonton fought off a few desperate attacks from the Flyers. When the clock hit zero, the whole team rushed onto the ice. The celebration was on.

Wayne hugged his teammates and gave them high fives. But he had something more special in mind for his celebration. When the Stanley Cup came onto the ice, he grabbed it and immediately skated over to Steve Smith. Wayne knew how badly Smith had felt after his blunder in the 1986 playoffs. He wanted the young defenseman to be the first to raise the cup for the fans.

"It was the hardest Cup we have won," Wayne said after the game. "I thought we played seven good games of hockey. This was by far the biggest game I've ever played. It could have been a great summer or the longest summer of my life."

After the playoff disaster of 1986, the Oilers were back on top of the hockey world. Wayne's life was good, but it was about to get a lot better. His fame and natural shyness had always made it difficult for him to have serious relationships with women. But in 1987, that changed. He was at a Los Angeles Lakers basketball game with friends when a twenty-four-year-old actress named Janet Jones came over to say hello. Wayne had met Janet several times before, but this time was different. The two felt an immediate attraction. They went out after the game with Wayne's friends and soon fell in love.

JANET JONES

Actress and dancer Janet Jones got her career started by winning the Miss Dance America contest at age sixteen. She appeared as a dancer in several movies during the early 1980s before getting her first big role in the 1984 film *The Flamingo Kid*. Her other popular films include *Police Academy 5* and *A League of Their Own*.

Wayne and Janet spent all the time they could together in the summer of 1987, but Wayne also had some hockey to play. It was time again for the Canada Cup, and Wayne was a key part of the Canadian team. As great as the 1987 Stanley Cup finals had been, the quality of play at the Canada Cup might have been even better. The Canadian roster read like an NHL all-star team. The roster was so loaded that the team was turning away some of the NHL's finest players.

Canada's biggest competition was the Soviet Union, which had a powerful, experienced national team. As expected, Canada and the Soviets met in the finals. The best-of-three series was hockey at its finest, with one tight, well-played game after another. In game one, Wayne led Canada to a big comeback. After trailing 4–1, the Canadian team blazed ahead 5–4.

But the Soviets quickly tied the game at 5–5 on a defensive mistake by Wayne and went on to win in overtime.

Wayne would later describe game two as the greatest game he'd ever played in. It was also one of the most exciting. The teams fought back and forth. Early on, Wayne wasn't shooting much, but he set up his teammates with three assists. With time running out, Canada led 5–4. But with less than two minutes to play, the Soviets tied the game. *Overtime!*

In the overtime session of game two of the 1987 Canada Cup finals, Wayne was so exhausted that he was losing control of his muscles. During a brief rest on the bench, he wet his pants. But nobody could tell, so he just went back onto the ice as if nothing had happened.

Wayne gave everything he had in the overtime session. If Canada lost, the series was over. By the end of the extra twenty-minute period, he was exhausted. But nobody had scored in the first overtime. The game was headed to double overtime! In that second extra session, Wayne was spending his fiftieth minute on the ice when he tipped a pass to Mario Lemieux, who put the puck in the back of the Soviet net to win the game. Wayne was so tired that he fell down and lay on the ice for ten minutes.

"To play against the best players and to have the game that I had made [winning] even that much more special," Wayne said.

With the series tied 1–1, it all came down to the third game. At first, the Soviets dominated, building a 3–0 lead. But Canada came back. By the third period, they'd tied the game 5–5. It looked like yet another overtime session was on its way.

Wayne was too sore and tired for another overtime. He was determined to win the cup in regulation. After a face-off, Wayne controlled the puck at the blue line. He noticed a breakdown in the Soviet defense and charged. Just like that, Canada was on its way to a three-on-one breakaway. Wayne faked a pass to Larry Murphy on his far right, then dropped the puck to Lemieux in the middle of the zone. Lemieux fired a rocket into the net. Canada was ahead! They held the Soviets off in the closing seconds and celebrated another Canada Cup. With three goals and eighteen assists, Wayne was the Canada Cup MVP. He couldn't celebrate for long, though. The NHL season was just a month away.

With three Stanley Cups in four years, the Oilers had high expectations for the 1987–1988 season. But from early on, cracks in the dynasty were beginning to show. Coach Sather had a tough, no-nonsense approach. That strict style worked well with a young team. But now, the Oilers were mostly accomplished veterans. They bristled at the treatment. Wayne and several other stars had public disputes with their coach. Even worse for Wayne was his contract situation. The Oilers wanted him to extend his deal, but Wayne wasn't ready for that yet.

MARIO LEMIEUX

As Wayne's skills slowly diminished with age, most hockey fans looked to Pittsburgh's Mario Lemieux to take his place as hockey's greatest player. Lemieux, born in Montreal in 1965, played a total of seventeen injury-plagued seasons for the Penguins. His finest season was 1988–1989, when his 199 points left him just shy of Wayne's exclusive 200-point club. Injuries and a battle with cancer robbed Lemieux of much of his playing time. Fans can only wonder if a healthy Lemieux could have chased down some of Wayne's records.

Still, the players and coaches were professionals. Once on the ice, they did their jobs. Coffey had been traded to Pittsburgh, but the rest of the team's core was intact. That was enough. It wasn't the greatest season for Wayne statistically. He had just 149 points on 40 goals and 109 assists. But he did hit a couple of milestones. In November, he became the second NHL player to get 1,000 career assists. In March, he broke Howe's assist record of 1,049.

Wayne also achieved a milestone in his personal life early in 1988. He proposed to Janet. She accepted, and the couple began planning a summer wedding. A few months later, the couple learned that Janet was pregnant. Wayne was going to be a husband *and* a father!

Injuries were part of the reason Wayne's numbers dipped in 1987–1988. He sat out sixteen games with a knee injury. The stretch was the first significant playing time he'd missed in his career. The time off the ice was also a big factor in the end of his MVP streak. Lemieux won the Hart Trophy.

The important thing, however, was the playoffs. Despite the team's struggles on and off the ice, the Oilers finished the season with the league's third-best record. They opened the playoffs with a 4–1 series victory over Winnipeg.

The next series was a highly anticipated matchup with the Flames. Wayne considered Calgary to be Edmonton's biggest competition for the Stanley Cup. In game one, he broke free of the Flame defense and scored a goal that bounced off the goalie's glove. The Oilers won, 3–1. Then in game two, the Oilers won on a short-handed goal in overtime. Edmonton was just trying to kill a penalty to get back to five-on-five hockey, but Wayne stole the puck and streaked down the ice. At the blue line, he drew back his stick and rifled a shot on goal. It was a surprising play to everyone on the ice—including Wayne's own teammates. Wayne rarely shot from so far out. But if the shot surprised his teammates, it surprised the Calgary goaltender even more. The high, hard one-timer sailed over his shoulder into the upper corner of the net. Game over! The series moved to Edmonton. With momentum on their side, the Oilers completed the series sweep.

After dominating Detroit 4–1, the Oilers advanced to the Stanley Cup finals. There, they would face the Boston Bruins. Wayne was worried about the Bruins. One reason was their tiny rink—the smallest in the NHL. Wayne preferred larger, more open rinks, which favored his speed and vision. Second, the Bruins played great physical defense, especially against Wayne. He knew that his work was cut out for him.

Despite Wayne's concerns, the Oilers were the clear favorites. They showed the Bruins why, winning the first three games and taking a commanding lead in the series. Game four in Boston started normally, but an electrical failure during the second period forced the NHL to cancel the game and move it to Edmonton. The second game four was close early on. But when Wayne assisted on a goal to give Edmonton a 4–2 lead, there was no looking back. The Oilers went on to a 6–3 win and a second straight Stanley Cup—their fourth in five years.

Wayne celebrated once again with his teammates and coaches. The Oilers had had their problems that year, but in the playoffs, they'd posted a remarkable 16–2 record. They were the most dominant team the league had seen in decades and a true sports dynasty. So when Wayne peeled off his number 99 Oilers jersey in the locker room after the game, nobody could have guessed that it was the last time he'd ever wear it.

Wayne Gretzky grew up playing hockey in Brantford, Ontario, Canada. He began skating when he was just two years old and played on many different teams as a child.

Wayne played for the Edmonton Oilers from 1978 to 1988. He won the World Hockey Association's Rookie of the Year award in 1979. The next year, the Oilers joined the National Hockey League (NHL).

Wayne and the Oilers won their first Stanley Cup in 1984 and followed it up with wins in 1985, 1987, and 1988.

Wayne joined the Los Angeles Kings in 1988. As a King, he scored his record-setting 802nd NHL goal against the Vancouver Canucks on March 23, 1994.

Wayne *(left)* was traded to the St. Louis Blues in 1995. He spent only part of one year with the team.

Wayne played for the Canadian hockey team at the 1998 Olympics in Nagano, Japan. The Canadians didn't play as well as expected and lost to Finland, 3–2, in the bronze-medal game.

Wayne waved good-bye after his final professional game on April 18, 1999, at Madison Square Garden. He spent the last three years of his career playing for the New York Rangers.

Wayne spoke to the crowd gathered to witness his induction into the Hockey Hall of Fame in Toronto, Canada, on November 22, 1999. Normally players have to wait three years before they are eligible for the Hall of Fame, but officials made an exception for Wayne.

Wayne stands with his wife, Janet Jones, and three of their children in 1999.

Wayne became part-owner of the Phoenix Coyotes in 2000. In 2005 he also became the team's head coach.

Chapter | Six

Change in the Air

At the beginning of the summer of 1988, twenty-seven-year-old Wayne was on top of the world. He was the star of the league's best team. He was marrying the woman he loved, and they were preparing to become parents.

Wayne and Janet had decided to have their wedding in Edmonton. That might have been a mistake. It was a media circus. By the time the big day—June 16—came, the press was calling it "Canada's Royal Wedding." The guest list topped seven hundred people. Another two hundred members of the media were there. And thousands of fans gathered outside. Despite the distractions, the couple had a good time. They didn't want all the extra attention, but they didn't let it spoil their day.

"It was a tough wedding because we had to try to satisfy not only friends and family, we had to satisfy fans, try to satisfy the media," Wayne said.

Actor and comedian Alan Thicke, a close friend of Wayne's, served as the master of ceremonies at Wayne and Janet's wedding.

After the wedding, things truly started to get crazy. Outrageous rumors about Wayne's future in Edmonton were swirling. Wayne was under contract for another year. He'd played his whole NHL career in Edmonton. The Oilers were the Stanley Cup champions and one of the league's all-time dynasties. Why would anyone mess with such a good thing?

But Oilers owner Peter Pocklington was having money troubles. Wayne was drawing a big salary. The trade rumors kept growing. Wayne said that he didn't want to go. (Pocklington insisted at the time that Wayne was demanding a trade.) He and Janet were set to buy a house in Edmonton. But soon, it became apparent that his future was out of his hands.

Once word got out that the Great Gretzky was available, trade offers came pouring in. One team, the Los Angeles Kings, was always at the center of the rumors. The Kings made Pocklington a huge offer—two players, three future first-round draft picks, and $15 million in exchange for Wayne and two other Oilers. Pocklington accepted the offer. The unthinkable had happened. The defending Stanley Cup champions had just traded the greatest player in the history of the game. Wayne Gretzky was no longer an Oiler.

The trade was announced at an August 9 press conference. Wayne tearfully said good-bye to the loyal Oiler fans. The Edmonton fans were crushed, as were many hockey fans across Canada. Many considered Wayne a national treasure, and now he'd be playing for a U.S. team.

Wayne's trade was huge news all across Canada. It was the front-page headline on most of the country's newspapers. In one newspaper, the size of the headline was bigger than any other headline the paper had run since the end of World War II in 1945.

"At that point, I felt like everyone else," Wayne said of the trade. "I couldn't believe it was happening. It wasn't as if we had just lost. We had just won the Stanley Cup for the fourth time in five years. I'd had, arguably, my best playoff ever. I won the [MVP], and all of a sudden, I'm traded."

That fall, Wayne reported to his new team. His presence sent ticket sales in Los Angeles skyrocketing. The team's average home attendance that year increased by more than three thousand fans. Los Angeles had never been a big hockey city, but the people knew who Wayne Gretzky was. The problem, however, was that many expected Wayne to singlehandedly make the Kings a new dynasty. The Kings hadn't been a powerhouse before the trade, and the team had given up a lot to get Wayne. That left a supporting cast that didn't come close to matching what Wayne had had in Edmonton. The league's all-time assist leader needed team-mates who could take advantage of his great passing and all of the attention opposing defenses gave him. Just adding Wayne wasn't going to be enough.

---

66 *I don't think we can justify the reasons why this happened. But we're all trying to do something that's good for Wayne, for the Edmonton Oilers, [and] for the National Hockey League.* 99

—GLEN SATHER ON THE TRADE

Still, having Wayne on the ice gave any team a fighting chance. On his first shot as a King, he gave the fans a reason to cheer. With a two-man advantage, winger Dave Taylor slid a quick pass to Wayne right in front of the net. Wayne popped the puck in for an easy goal. The Los Angeles crowd roared, excited about their new superstar. Wayne gave them more reasons to cheer as he added three assists in the victory.

It was a good start, and a hot streak followed. The Kings won their first four games of the season. Hockey had never been more popular in Los Angeles. People jokingly called it *Hockeywood* (since Hollywood is so close to Los Angeles). The Kings played a wide-open, offensive style. It made for a lot of high scores and highlight-reel goals. But on the flip side, the team's defense wasn't always up to the task. Still, the formula was working and the Kings were an improved team.

On October 19, Wayne suited up for the game he'd been dreading from the moment the schedule had come out. It was his return to Edmonton. As he stepped onto the ice in another team's jersey, he didn't know what to expect. Would his old fans boo him? He was ready for that, but it would have hurt him. But from the moment he came out, the fan reaction was clear. They gave him a standing ovation. They remembered all the good times and let him know how much they appreciated his years as an Oiler. Wayne was touched by the reception. He'd had problems with Pocklington and Sather, but his relationship with the fans still meant a lot to him.

On the ice, Wayne met his old friend Mark Messier. It wasn't a friendly greeting, though. During the game, Messier checked Wayne hard into the boards, then did it again later on. They would always be friends off the ice, but on it, Messier wanted to flatten number 99. He got his wish. He flattened Wayne, and the Oilers flattened the Kings, 8–6. Wayne was just glad the game was over.

Two months later, Wayne had much better news. On December 19, Janet gave birth to a healthy baby girl, Paulina Mary Jean Gretzky.

The Kings finished the season at 42-31-7. In Edmonton, that record would have been a sore disappointment. But for Los Angeles, it gave fans reason to hope. Wayne had tallied 168 points on 54 goals and 114 assists. He'd also reclaimed the Hart Trophy as the league's MVP. Now it was time to see if the Kings could do anything in the playoffs.

Fate was cruel to Wayne, however. The Kings' first-round opponent was his old team—the defending Stanley Cup champs. The Kings and Oilers split the first two games in Los Angeles. Then it was back to Edmonton. For years, Wayne had made other teams fear playing the Oilers there. But now, he was on the visiting bench.

The Oilers were fired up. Many experts had predicted that they would struggle without Wayne. They were eager to prove that they were still a force, and that's exactly what they did. They won game three, 3–0, then took game four when Messier broke a 3–3 tie with less than a minute to go.

Even after the losses, Wayne remained confident. The Kings bounced back to win game five, 4–2, then took game six, 4–1. The series was knotted at three.

Game seven was in Los Angeles. Fans filled the arena with a level of excitement Los Angeles hockey had never seen before. And when Wayne scored just fifty-two seconds into the game, the excitement only grew.

As many of the Kings' games had been that season, game seven was a high-scoring, back-and-forth affair. Late in the second period, Wayne and the Kings broke it open by taking a 5–3 lead. Wayne later added an empty-net goal to seal the win. The Kings had won three games in a row to knock out the defending champions. Wayne was advancing to the second round, while his old teammates were going home. In Edmonton, the fans were angrier than ever at Pocklington. They accused him of selling Wayne and destroying a dynasty all for a bit of cash.

The thrilling comeback win in the first round was the highlight of the year for Los Angeles. It was also their *last* highlight. Calgary swept the Kings in the second round. Los Angeles had shown improvement. But for Wayne—who was used to titles, not second-round exits—the season ended far too early.

In 1989–1990, Wayne reminded his fans of his past brilliance by winning the league's scoring title—his first in three years. But that season his body also first showed signs of breaking down.

He missed five games at the end of the regular season with a back injury. Wayne's twenty-nine-year-old body had endured the punishment of professional hockey for twelve seasons, and he was beginning to pay the price.

Wayne had a simple strategy when big fights broke out and the whole team got in on it. He'd grab the smallest guy on the other team. They'd just hold on to each other and make it look like they were fighting. But most of the time, they'd just be acting.

Despite the pains, Wayne's playing was fantastic. He was chasing down another of the NHL's greatest records—Gordie Howe's 1,850 career points. Wayne actually had mixed emotions about breaking another one of his idol's records, but he was so close entering the year that it was only a matter of time. Almost as if by fate, he broke the record in Edmonton.

Howe was at the game. So was Wayne's family. The game before, Wayne had scored a game-winning goal against Vancouver with one second left on the clock. That goal had pulled Wayne to within one point of Howe's record.

Early in the game against the Oilers, Wayne got an assist to tie Howe. But in the second period, his ex-teammate Jeff Beukeboom crushed Wayne with a huge check. Rattled, Wayne spent some time on the bench recovering. Fans thought maybe the record would have to wait.

By late in the third period, Wayne was back on the ice. With the Kings trailing 4–3 and just three minutes left in the game, the fans started chanting his name. They were rooting for the Oilers, but they still wanted to see Wayne break the record in Edmonton.

The clock kept ticking. Soon, only a minute remained. That was when the Kings took control of the puck for one final attack. Wayne skated out in front of the net—not his usual spot. (He preferred to start a play behind the net.) A bad pass trickled away from the Kings' Taylor. It bounced right to Wayne's stick. Oiler goalie Bill Ranford hadn't expected the lucky bounce. He was out of position, and Wayne poked a backhanded shot into the net. The record-breaking goal tied the game at 4–4. Excited, Wayne jumped into the arms of his teammates. The arena erupted—one of the rare moments when fans have cheered the loss of their team's lead.

The officials stopped the game. Howe came onto the ice, along with Wayne's family. Messier presented Wayne with a diamond bracelet from the Oilers. He also got gifts from the Kings and the NHL.

"This is the greatest feeling in the world," Wayne told the cheering crowd. He fought back tears, knowing that the game wasn't over yet.

As if Wayne's night wasn't already memorable enough, he had one more moment. In overtime, he slapped yet another backhanded shot past Ranford for the game winner. It was his second game-winning goal in two games. The exciting victory made his record-breaking point even more special.

"I actually think Wayne felt a little bad about breaking the record," Howe said. "That's the kind of kid he is. He wanted to do it and he had to do it. He couldn't go the rest of the season without any points. But he didn't want to see me hurt by it all."

Despite Wayne's individual heroics, the Kings struggled in 1989–1990, just barely making the playoffs. Although the Kings didn't have a great regular-season record, nobody wanted to be playing the Great Gretzky in the playoffs, even with his back injury.

Los Angeles's first-round opponent was Calgary, one of the NHL's best teams and the defending Stanley Cup champions. The Kings were heavy underdogs—something Wayne hadn't experienced in a decade. Worse still, Wayne's back hurt so much that he didn't even play in the first two games of the series. Somehow, the Kings earned a split even without their star. Wayne returned to the ice for game three. It was a huge lift for the Kings, and his early assist helped them to an overtime win.

With momentum on their side, the Kings crushed the Flames in game four, 12–4. Suddenly, they were one win away from a huge upset. After Calgary won game five, the Kings came back in game six. Down one goal in the third period, Wayne got an assist on the tying goal to send the game to overtime, then celebrated when Mike Krusher scored to give the Kings the series victory. For the second straight year, the Kings had knocked out the defending Stanley Cup champions in the first round.

In the second round, they faced the Oilers. Edmonton was hungry for revenge against the team that had brought their season to an end the previous year. The Kings, badly slowed by injuries, didn't have much of a fight left in them. Wayne played through the pain in his back until Steve Smith flattened him with a hard check in game three. Wayne's effort wasn't nearly enough. The Oilers swept the series. "As ecstatic as we were last year after beating Edmonton, I'm disappointed," Wayne said. "I hate losing."

The Oilers went on to win the Stanley Cup in 1990—their first without Wayne. They beat the Bruins 4–1.

Watching from the bench wasn't the way Wayne wanted to end the season. But in July 1990, the birth of his second child, Ty Robert, helped him get over the disappointment. Wayne's hockey career had changed a lot over the past two years, but his personal life had changed a lot more, and he couldn't have been happier.

Chapter Seven

A Different Gretzky

By the time the 1990–1991 season started, Wayne was twenty-nine years old. By normal standards, that wasn't old for a hockey player. But Wayne had been playing pro hockey since he was seventeen. On the great Oiler teams, he had usually played deep into the playoffs, which added up to a lot of extra punishment. His body was starting to show signs of wearing down.

Wayne's years of 200-point seasons were behind him. But even with a bad back, he was still the Great Gretzky. His 163 points in 1990–1991 was far short of his personal highs, but it was still good enough for the NHL's scoring title and the Art Ross Trophy.

The season was also filled with several personal milestones. Wayne became the first NHL player to score two thousand points in a career. He also joined a list of just four players to tally 700 career goals.

Better yet, the Kings were an improved team. They posted the league's third-best record and seemed poised for a big play-off run. For the first time since his arrival in Los Angeles, the team around Wayne was good enough to seriously challenge for the Stanley Cup.

❝ *I owe everything I have to hockey. It's given me . . . a chance to see the world, to meet some great people. I get paid a lot of money for something that I love to do. And when you think you're bigger than the sport, you're in trouble."*

—WAYNE GRETZKY

After falling behind 2–1 to Vancouver in the first round of the playoffs, Wayne and the Kings came storming back. They won the next three games to advance to the second round.

A familiar foe waited in the second round. For the third straight year, Wayne faced his former team in the playoffs. The series was surrounded by media hype. The Oilers were the defending champions, but Wayne's Kings would be a tough test.

The series started with all of the excitement fans had antic-ipated. Los Angeles took game one in overtime on a goal by Luc

Robitaille. The next two games went into overtime as well, but the Oilers managed to win both.

From there, Edmonton never looked back. They took games four and five to win the series. Wayne had played well in the playoffs, scoring fifteen points in the team's twelve games. But once again, the Kings came up short. Wayne was being reminded of just how hard it is to win in the playoffs.

The 1991–1992 season was a disappointment for Wayne and the Kings. Wayne led the league in assists with ninety, but he scored a career-low thirty-one goals. One of the season's few highlights was Wayne's 1,500th career assist, which came on March 4 against the San Jose Sharks. Los Angeles made the playoffs, where they once again faced the Oilers. But as in recent years, the Oilers handled the Kings, sending them home in six games.

In 1991 Wayne and Canadian actor John Candy bought the Toronto Argonauts of the Canadian Football League.

Before the 1992–1993 season, Wayne's back was hurting more than ever. He tried to play through the pain at training camp, but clearly something was very wrong. Doctors told him that he had a herniated disk in his back. One of the pads that cushions the spine had ruptured—a very painful injury. He might need as long as a year to recover and get back into playing shape.

To Wayne, missing a whole season wasn't acceptable. He worked hard to rehabilitate his body. He stayed in shape. He watched the Kings' first thirty-nine games of the season. Surprisingly, the team was doing well even without their star center. Luc Robitaille led the Kings' attack, with help from new addition Jari Kurri. On January 6, 1993, Wayne returned to the ice far ahead of schedule. He assisted on two goals in his first game, then scored two himself in his second. Wayne was back.

 On September 14, 1992, Janet and Wayne had their third child, Trevor Douglas.

Wayne continued his fantastic play throughout the second half of the season. With sixty-five points on sixteen goals and forty-nine assists, he showed no ill effects of his injury.

The Kings' first-round playoff opponent was Calgary. The Kings entered the postseason on a hot streak, and that momentum carried into the first round. In the team's 4–2 series win, they scored an amazing thirty-three goals. Next up was Vancouver—one of the NHL's best teams that year. Again, the Kings won the series in six games. The pivotal win came in a game-five over-time victory.

The Kings advanced to the conference finals, where they faced the Toronto Maple Leafs. On the ice, Wayne looked reju-venated, reminding fans of the Gretzky of old. But Toronto was a good team and took a 3–2 series lead with an overtime win in game five.

Game six was in Los Angeles. The arena was buzzing with excitement and nervousness. If Toronto won, the series was over. The fans and players were on edge as the game went into overtime, tied 4–4. But in the overtime session, Wayne gave the fans reason to cheer with a thrilling power-play goal. The series was headed back to Toronto for a deciding game seven.

Wayne was determined to return to the Stanley Cup finals. He'd grown up near Toronto, and the city felt almost like home to him. He didn't intend to let his season end in front of his fam-ily and friends. "I knew that no matter what I've done in the city of Toronto over my career, if we don't win game seven, people are always going to remember that," he said.

Wayne didn't let the chance slip away. He dominated the ice, scoring two early goals and adding an assist. But despite his stellar performance, the Kings were clinging to a one-goal lead.

In the third period, Wayne controlled the puck near the Toronto goal. His defender stuck to him, giving him no open shots. Wayne skated with the puck behind the net and fought through the defensive pressure. He reached around and slid the puck out in front of the net. A centering pass in that situation is a common play. Wayne was just hoping that a teammate could get a stick on the puck. But instead, the puck hit a Toronto player's skate and bounced back into the net. Wayne had scored his third goal of the game and his fourth point. The Kings went on to a 5–4 victory and earned a trip to the Stanley Cup finals for the first time in Kings history.

Wayne had won four Stanley Cups during his years in Edmonton. After five seasons in Los Angeles, he'd worked hard to achieve this finals berth. "I don't think I've ever had as much personal satisfaction," he said of the win over the Maple Leafs.

The Canadiens awaited the Kings in the Stanley Cup finals. The Kings were hot, but Montreal was hotter. They'd cruised through the playoffs and had had plenty of time off as the Kings and Maple Leafs battled to seven games. Montreal was well rested, giving them a huge advantage. Still, the Kings held on to their momentum with a 4–1 victory in the series opener.

In game two, everything started to fall apart. The Kings had a one-goal lead in the game when Montreal coach Jacques Demers asked the referee to check the stick of Los Angeles defenseman Marty McSorley. The referee determined that McSorley was using a stick with an illegal curvature and awarded the Canadiens a power play. (Sticks with a greater curvature can increase the power and accuracy of shots, giving players an unfair advantage as well as causing safety concerns. NHL rules at this time allowed a maximum curvature of one-half inch.) Montreal converted to tie the game, then went on to win it in overtime. The Kings had seemed poised to take a commanding 2–0 series lead, but suddenly the series was knotted at one game apiece.

This team wasn't supposed to win. We weren't the best team. We were just a hard-working team that believed in each other . . . and we wanted to win for the next guy beside us.

—WAYNE GRETZKY ON THE 1992–1993 KINGS

Games three and four were in Los Angeles, but the Kings were unable to take advantage of the home ice, losing both games in overtime. In game five in Montreal, the Canadiens skated to an easy 4–1 win to claim the Stanley Cup.

NHL Top Single-Season Point Totals

1. 215, Wayne Gretzky, 1985–1986
2. 212, Wayne Gretzky, 1981–1982
3. 208, Wayne Gretzky, 1984–1985
4. 205, Wayne Gretzky, 1983–1984
5. 199, Mario Lemieux, 1988–1989

The season had been a great run for the Kings. Wayne had scored forty points on fifteen goals and twenty-five assists in the playoffs. But his frustration at losing in the finals left Wayne questioning whether he wanted to continue playing. For the first time, he began to think seriously about retiring. He just wasn't sure how many more seasons his body and emotions could endure.

Chapter Eight

The Final Seasons

Despite the nagging injuries and the finals disappointment of 1993, Wayne was back on the ice with the Kings in 1993–1994. As the season progressed, everyone was watching number 99. He was nearing the last big record that wasn't yet his—Howe's 801 career goals. By early January, Wayne was approaching that number. Fans and the media started to follow him closely, knowing he might soon break Howe's record.

The buildup to breaking the record was difficult for Wayne. In January, his house was badly damaged by an earthquake that struck Southern California. On March 4, his good friend and business partner John Candy died of a heart attack. With all the off-ice distractions, Wayne was having a hard time scoring. During one stretch, he scored just one point in seven games.

Wayne finally broke the record in Los Angeles on March 23, 1994, in a game against Vancouver. In the second period, he took a pass from McSorley and fired a wrist shot from the left side of the goal. The puck sailed past the goalie into the back of the net—number 802 of Wayne's amazing career. The officials stopped the game so that Wayne's parents and Janet could join him on the ice for a ceremony. "[Hockey is] the greatest game in the world," Wayne told the Vancouver crowd. "And I feel great that I play in the NHL."

❝[802 goals] was a record that nobody thought would ever be broken. . . . So when I scored the goal, it was almost overwhelming to me.❞

—WAYNE GRETZKY

Even though the Kings missed the playoffs in 1993–1994, Wayne was feeling good. He was on his way to his tenth career scoring title (he scored 130 points that season), and late in the season he signed a new three-year, $25.5-million deal with the Kings. The retirement talk was a thing of the past. Wayne was ready to play on.

The 1994–1995 season got off to a rough start. NHL players and owners periodically negotiate a collective bargaining agreement (CBA). The CBA covers all aspects of the players' employment, including issues like salary caps, the freedom of the players to become free agents, and much more. When the two sides couldn't agree on the CBA, the owners began canceling games.

To fill the time, Wayne started a team of his own, which he called the Ninety-Nine All-Stars. The team, which included his friend Mark Messier, played national teams from other countries. The games were a good way to stay in shape and give hockey fans something to watch while the league and players settled their differences. The games showed that, for most players, professional hockey wasn't just about the money.

BRENT GRETZKY

Wayne's younger brother Brent also loved hockey. While Brent didn't have quite the talent of his older, more famous brother, he spent many seasons in hockey's minor leagues. In 1992 he was drafted by the Tampa Bay Lightning of the NHL. He played thirteen games for the Lightning from 1993 to 1995, scoring one goal and adding three assists.

The shortened NHL season held few highlights for Wayne and his Kings. Once again, Los Angeles struggled and missed the playoffs. Wayne scored 11 goals and 48 points, including his 2,500th career point in April of 1995. But on the whole, 1994–1995 was forgettable for Wayne, the Kings, and the entire NHL.

Wayne entered the 1995–1996 season at thirty-four years of age. When the Kings stumbled to yet another poor start, trade rumors began flying once again. Wayne knew that his time in the league was running out, and he badly wanted to play for a contending team. Since Los Angeles's loss in the Stanley Cup finals in 1994, Wayne hadn't even been to the playoffs. If he stayed with the Kings, it didn't look like he'd be back anytime soon.

The New York Rangers were at the center of most of the trade rumors. Messier played for the Rangers, and the idea of reuniting Wayne with his former teammate appealed to many hockey fans. But in a surprise move, the Kings traded their star center to the St. Louis Blues instead. On February 28, 1996, the Blues sent Los Angeles three players and two future draft choices for Wayne.

"I'm ecstatic," Wayne said about the trade. "I'm thrilled to be going [to St. Louis]. It's going to be exciting."

The Blues were in a race for a playoff spot, and team officials hoped that Wayne's talent and experience would help push them deep into the playoffs. Wayne's time with the Blues started off with a bang—literally. In his second game with St. Louis, an elbow to his head knocked him to the ice. He left the game with a concussion (a brain injury caused by a blow to the head) and missed the next several games because of it. But when he did return, he helped the Blues skate to a playoff berth, scoring twenty-one points in eighteen regular-season games.

In the playoffs, Wayne helped spark the underdog Blues to a series win over the Toronto Maple Leafs. The series was closely contested, with three of the six games going into overtime. Another exciting series followed in the second round, when the Blues and the Detroit Red Wings battled to a decisive game seven. The winner would advance to the conference finals. The game was a physical, defensive struggle. Neither team scored in regulation, so the teams headed into overtime. After twenty minutes of overtime play, the score was still 0–0. But finally, in double overtime, Detroit's Steve Yzerman ended St. Louis's hopes with a series-clinching goal. In the Blues' thirteen playoff games, Wayne had scored sixteen points.

Wayne's career in St. Louis was brief. After the 1995–1996 season, the thirty-five-year-old center was a free agent. He could sign with whatever team he chose. That off-season, Wayne was the talk of the league. Fans knew that his career was nearing an end. Which team would he sign with? Would it be the last team of his career? Some hoped he would return to Edmonton, or at least to Canada, to end his career. But on July 22, 1996, Wayne announced that he had signed a two-year, $8-million contract with the New York Rangers. After all the trade talk earlier that year, Wayne would finally be reuniting with Messier in New York.

"It was a tough decision," Wayne said. "I guess probably what tipped the scales was the chance to play with Mark [Messier] and the opportunity to get a chance to play with a team that is really focused on trying to win a championship."

MARK MESSIER

Wayne called Mark Messier the best player he ever played with. Messier, nicknamed "Moose," was born in St. Albert, Alberta, in 1961. He and Gretzky formed a powerful combination in Edmonton. When Wayne left the team, Messier took his friend's place as the Oilers' star. Messier took his magic to New York in 1991 and led the Rangers to a Stanley Cup title in 1994. He also spent time with the Vancouver Canucks before returning to New York to retire in 2004.

Before the season started, however, Wayne had another chance to represent his country. The Canada Cup had been replaced by the World Cup of Hockey, and Canada was one of the favorites to win. Wayne was once again the team captain.

Because Messier was also on the team, the old teammates got a head start playing together. Their old head coach, Glen Sather, was even there. He said of the two, "They were like a couple of teenagers. . . . They were like a couple of brothers who hadn't seen each other in a long, long time."

Canada wasn't able to capture the World Cup, though. After defeating Sweden 3–2 in double overtime in the semifinals, Canada lost to the United States two games to one in the finals. Wayne was his team's leading scorer with seven points in eight games.

In the fall of 1996, Wayne reported to the Rangers. Playing with an old friend on a new team rejuvenated Wayne. He tied for fourth in the league scoring race with ninety-seven points on twenty-five goals and seventy-two assists. Messier, meanwhile, scored eighty-four points. Together they led the Rangers to the playoffs.

New York's first-round opponent was the Florida Panthers. Despite dropping the first game 3–0, the Rangers won the series 4–1. One of the series highlights for Wayne was the fourth game, in which he scored a hat trick.

In the second round, the Rangers faced the New Jersey Devils. The Rangers lost the first game 2–0, then came back to win the next four games. But the conference finals were a different story. The Rangers faced the Flyers, and Philadelphia dominated the older Rangers, taking the series in five games. It was a good run for Wayne, Messier, and the Rangers, but they'd come up short.

The next two seasons, 1997–1998 and 1998–1999, were unremarkable for the Rangers. Messier left the team for Vancouver in 1997. Many critics pointed out that the team was too old and that the Rangers couldn't build a team around a star in his late thirties. While the fans enjoyed watching the hockey legend on the ice, the game plan wasn't a winning formula. New York missed the playoffs both seasons.

Wayne did have some personal highlights, though. On October 11, 1997, he got two early goals against Vancouver. He was a goal away from his fiftieth career hat trick. Soon, he had the puck and was charging down the ice. He skated right at two Vancouver defenders and faked a shot. Both defenders dove to block the shot. But Wayne held the puck, skated to the right side of the goal, and faked again. The goalie dove, but Wayne wrapped around behind the net and easily deposited the puck into the undefended goal. He'd faked out three Canucks in one of the most amazing goals of his long career.

In 1998 Wayne was selected to the Canadian Winter Olympic hockey team. It was the first year NHL players had been allowed to compete. Despite starting out 3–0, Team Canada didn't make it to the gold-medal game. They lost to Finland for the bronze. It was a bitter disappointment for the Canadian players and fans.

By the spring of 1999, Wayne knew his career was coming to a close. He didn't want to be an athlete who holds on too long, staying in the sport long after it has passed him by. And he'd enjoyed some nice moments that year, including being named the MVP of the NHL All-Star Game. At the end of the season, he even broke yet another of Howe's records when he scored the 1,072nd goal of his professional career (Howe had scored 1,071, counting playoff games and his days in the WHA). Wayne had proved that he still belonged in the NHL. But he was ready to walk away. It was time to retire.

Wayne broke Howe's goals record in just his 1,117th career game. By comparison, Howe needed 1,767 games to reach that total.

As the season neared its end, the Rangers were out of the playoff hunt. Fans could only wonder if they were watching Wayne's final games. On April 15, the Rangers were in Ottawa to play the Senators. Everyone knew that this was probably Wayne's last game in Canada, even though he hadn't yet made his official announcement. After the game ended in a 2–2 tie, the Foo Fighters song "My Hero" played over the arena's public address system. The fans stood and cheered long after the final buzzer sounded, forcing Wayne to return to the ice three times.

"[On the third time out] that's when it hit me that I'm retired," Wayne said. "Up until then it's in your mind. You know it's going to happen and you're thinking about it, but that's when it first hit me that I was done."

The next day, Wayne made his retirement official. He had one game left to play, on April 18 against the Pittsburgh Penguins. On the way to the game, he rode with his dad. In the car, Walter was still trying to talk his son out of retiring. Many fans felt the same way. But Wayne was confident in his decision. He'd had a long, successful career. It was time to move on to the next phase of his life.

❝I probably miss the game more than the game misses Wayne Gretzky. Nothing can replace hockey. It was my life for thirty-six years.**❞**

—WAYNE GRETZKY

The game itself was exciting, but it wasn't a storybook ending for Wayne. The Penguins won in overtime. In the locker room afterward, Wayne had mixed emotions. A photographer snapped a famous photo of him taking off his skates for the last time. He didn't take off the rest of his equipment for two hours. Wayne found it hard to leave the locker room.

"I feel so lucky to be able to play in the NHL," Wayne told reporters. "I've been so fortunate to play with some of the greatest players, against guys I admired so much, like the best player I ever played against, Mario Lemieux . . . my teammates and, of course, the best player I ever played with, Mark Messier."

Chapter | Nine

Behind the Glass

even months after his retirement, Wayne received a special honor. Normally, no player can be inducted into the Hockey Hall of Fame in Toronto until he's been retired for at least three years. But the Hall of Fame waived that rule for Wayne. After all, he was the Great Gretzky. A crowd of 2,500 fans packed the Hall to see Wayne's induction.

"I felt so fortunate to be part of this game," he said in his speech. "I felt like a kid every day."

The NHL didn't stop there, though. At the 2000 All-Star Game, the league retired Wayne's number, 99. No other NHL player will ever wear that number.

"It was an honor he richly deserved," said NHL commissioner Gary Bettman. "It was kind of easy because I can't imagine anybody ever putting on that number. . . . It is a great honor to a great individual who deserves it."

Wayne's life changed drastically after he retired, both personally and professionally. In 2000 Janet gave birth to the couple's fourth child, Tristan Wayne. Three years later, a fifth child, Emma Marie, was born. But Wayne never left the game of hockey behind. He was done as a player, but not as a participant.

In the summer of 2000, Wayne was back in hockey news again. He'd teamed up with Steve Ellman, who was buying the NHL's Phoenix Coyotes. Gretzky would be a part owner of the team and would take charge of the team's hockey operations. At first, rumors swirled about Wayne also taking over as the Coyote head coach. But Wayne insisted that wasn't going to happen. He didn't want to coach, he said. He'd leave that up to someone else.

THE PHOENIX COYOTES

The Phoenix Coyotes organization started out as the Winnipeg Jets of the WHA. Along with Edmonton and two other WHA teams, the Jets joined the NHL in 1979. But the team struggled in Winnipeg, and new owners finally moved the team to Phoenix in 1996. The organization has continued its struggles there. It's the oldest NHL team never to have appeared in a Stanley Cup final.

That same year, Wayne also took over the management of Team Canada. He helped select the players and coaches that would go to Salt Lake City, Utah, for the 2002 Winter Olympics.

Team Canada had suffered several disappointments in recent international competitions, and the country was eager for a winner. But when the team started out poorly, Wayne and the rest of the team took a lot of criticism from reporters and fans. Wayne lashed out at the media. He told them not to judge the team so quickly.

A rivalry soon grew between Wayne and U.S. hockey fans. Wayne accused U.S. fans of taking pleasure in Canada's struggles. The fans replied by calling Wayne a crybaby. But in the end, Wayne and Team Canada got the last laugh. Team Canada beat the United States 5–2 in the gold-medal game, giving Canada its first Olympic gold in fifty years. Once again, Wayne was a hero to Canadian hockey fans everywhere.

In 2003 Wayne briefly returned to the ice with some of his old Oiler teammates for an exhibition game against retired members of the Montreal Canadiens. The game was part of a celebration of the Oilers' twenty-fifth anniversary as a team.

Wayne enjoyed running the Coyotes. But the NHL was in bad shape after a long, difficult labor disagreement between the owners and the players in 2004–2005. The entire season was canceled, and the league badly needed to rekindle fan interest for the 2005–2006 season. Wayne stepped up, announcing that he would take over as the head coach of the Coyotes. The NHL's greatest player was ready to try his luck on the other side of the glass. His decision was a big boost to fixing the league's damaged reputation.

"I'll be honest with you . . . I never thought I'd be a coach in the NHL," Wayne told reporters. "But I'm excited about the challenge. . . . The last couple of weeks I've been following my son's baseball team around and I kind of got the itch to coach, as silly as that sounds."

Wayne finally got his chance on October 5 in the season opener, but the Vancouver Canucks beat Phoenix 3–2. Three nights later, however, Wayne got his first win as a head coach, 2–1 over the Minnesota Wild. (The North Stars moved to Dallas, Texas, in 1993. The Wild entered the league as an expansion team in 2000.)

Although the Coyotes went on to finish in last place in the tough Pacific Division in 2005–2006, many fans were encouraged. Many experts expected the Coyotes to be one of the league's worst teams. But they stayed in playoff contention for much of the season, before fading late.

Wayne's greatest disappointments during the season, however, had nothing to do with the Coyotes. Late in 2005, his mother died of lung cancer. Then, shortly before the 2006 Winter Olympics, when Wayne was again directing Team

Canada, Janet was caught up in a public gambling scandal. She and a group of others had been involved in a gambling ring that was making large bets on sporting events.

---

66 *Hockey will always be number two to my family. And to me, friends are more important than business."*

—WAYNE GRETZKY

For most people, accusations of gambling on sports wouldn't be that big of a deal. But for the wife of an NHL coach, it was a major news story. Wayne stood by Janet during this difficult period, though time and again he denied ever having anything to do with the gambling ring. Investigators agreed that Wayne hadn't been involved. But the scandal was enough to make some people question him. Having to defend himself repeatedly for something he'd never done was tough.

Wayne had hoped the 2006 Winter Olympics would overshadow the gambling rumors. But what he saw from Team Canada on the ice did little to make him feel better. The Canadians appeared outmatched. They lost to Russia in the quarterfinals and didn't even get to play for a medal. Wayne, as the architect of the team, took heavy criticism for many of his choices.

"I'll take all the responsibility for not winning," he said. "We're not going to go anywhere. This country will regroup and this team will be ready for 2010." Wayne wouldn't say, however, whether he'd be back as the team director for the 2010 games in Vancouver.

With all the disappointments and frustrations of the previous year, many wondered if Wayne would be back to coach the Coyotes in 2006–2007. But in May, he answered those questions by signing a five-year deal to remain Phoenix's head coach. The forty-four-year-old told reporters that he wasn't satisfied with his job the previous season. He was anxious to guide Phoenix to a Stanley Cup.

❝ *It seems like just yesterday [Wayne] skated for the first time, and now he's finished. . . . I just can't find the words to describe how nice it is. And of course, we're so proud of Wayne, certainly of his hockey ability . . . but more so the person he is.* ❞

—WALTER GRETZKY

"I think that, had I walked away this year, I would not have been happy with what I'd accomplished as far as wins and losses went last year," he said. "The only way that you're remembered as an athlete and a coach is [for] winning championships. As well as I did as a player, I never went to another level until we won our first championship. And to me, that's the way it is coaching too." Only time will tell if Wayne the coach will ever reach the heights of Wayne the player.

Epilogue

The Great One

Fans of all sports like to debate their greatest athletes of all time. In golf, fans go back and forth between Tiger Woods and Jack Nicklaus. In baseball, the discussion includes Babe Ruth, Willie Mays, and Barry Bonds. In basketball, fans argue about Bill Russell, Wilt Chamberlain, and Michael Jordan. But with the way Wayne dominated the NHL for more than a decade, there's really no debate about hockey's all-time great. It's number 99. Stars like Howe, Esposito, and Lemieux are all fighting for recognition as a distant second.

Wayne brought star power and respectability to a sport that badly needed it. Long before he left Edmonton for Los Angeles, he was the worldwide face of hockey. He's been retired for years now, but if you ask most people to name a hockey player, Wayne Gretzky is the name that will come to their lips.

He has made a difference off the ice too. Wayne is eager to share his success, and he works with several charities. In 2000 he began hosting an annual golf tournament that has raised money to support a variety of children's charities. He has also started the Wayne Gretzky Foundation to help give disadvantaged kids the chance to play hockey.

In 1999 the ESPN television network released a list of the greatest athletes of the twentieth century. Gretzky was voted number five, behind Michael Jordan, Babe Ruth, Muhammad Ali, and Jim Brown. Although it's impossible to compare one sport to another, one thing is certain. None of those athletes dominated his sport quite the same way Gretzky did. Nobody else has assaulted the record books quite like Gretzky.

It's impossible to know whether anyone will challenge Wayne's many records. But even if someone does, what Wayne accomplished won't be diminished. He was born to play professional hockey. And for two decades, that's exactly what he did.

PERSONAL STATISTICS

Name:

Wayne Douglas Gretzky

Position:

Center

Nicknames:

The Great Gretzky, The Great One

Born:

January 26, 1961

Height:

6'0"

Weight:

180 lbs.

Residence:

Los Angeles, California

NHL STATISTICS

Season	Team	Games	Goals	Assists	Points	Penalty Minutes
1979–80	EDM	79	51	86	137	21
1980–81	EDM	80	55	109	164	28
1981–82	EDM	80	92	120	212	26
1982–83	EDM	80	71	125	196	59
1983–84	EDM	74	87	118	205	39
1984–85	EDM	80	73	135	208	52
1985–86	EDM	80	52	163	215	46
1986–87	EDM	79	62	121	183	28
1987–88	EDM	64	40	109	149	24
1988–89	LAK	78	54	114	168	26
1989–90	LAK	73	40	102	142	42
1990–91	LAK	78	41	122	163	16
1991–92	LAK	74	31	90	121	34
1992–93	LAK	45	16	49	65	6
1993–94	LAK	81	38	92	130	20
1994–95	LAK	48	11	37	48	6
1995–96	LAK/STL	80	23	79	102	34
1996–97	NYR	82	25	72	97	28
1997–98	NYR	82	23	67	90	28
1998–99	NYR	70	9	53	62	14
Career		1,487	894	1,963	2,857	577

CAREER PLAYOFF STATISTICS

Games	Goals	Assists	Points	Penalty Minutes
208	122	260	382	66

GLOSSARY

blue line: the line in hockey that separates each team's zone from center ice

check: to collide with another player, usually into the boards surrounding the rink

concussion: an injury to the brain resulting from a blow to the head

hat trick: three goals in a single game

merge: to combine two businesses or leagues into one

option: part of a contract that gives one party the choice on whether to extend the contract

points: goals plus assists

rookie: a first-year player

tonsillitis: an inflammation of the tonsils

zone: the area on each end of the ice, separated from center ice by a blue line

SOURCES

3   *Ultimate Gretzky 4-Disc Special Edition*, DVD (Los Angeles, CA: Insight Sports Ltd., NHL Productions, Warner Home Video, 2006).

4   *Ultimate Gretzky.*

7   Thomas R. Raber, *Wayne Gretzky: Hockey Great* (Minneapolis: Lerner Publications Company, 1991), 16.

10 Wayne Gretzky with Rick Reilly, *Gretzky: An Autobiography* (New York: HarperCollins, 1990), 20.

10 Jane Mersky Leder, *Wayne Gretzky* (Mankato, MN: Crestwood House, 1985), 9.

10 Gretzky, *Gretzky*, 22.

11 Andrew Podnieks, *The Great One: The Life and Times of Wayne Gretzky* (Chicago: Triumph Books, 1999), 8.

12 Raber, *Wayne Gretzky*, 20.

16 Ibid., 29.

20 Leder, *Wayne Gretzky*, 16.

22 Podnieks, *The Great One*, 76.

22 Jack Falla, "Wayne Gretzky: Greatness Ascendant," *NHL.com.*, n.d., http://www.nhl.com/hockeyu/ history/gretzky/greatnessascendant .html (September 1, 2006).

26 Leder, *Wayne Gretzky*, 22.

28 *Ultimate Gretzky.*

35 Ibid.

35 Leder, *Wayne Gretzky*, 34.

37 Raber, *Wayne Gretzky*, 34.

39 Gretzky, *Gretzky*, 78.

40 Raber, *Wayne Gretzky*, 34.

42 Leder, *Wayne Gretzky*, 35.

42 Gretzky, *Gretzky*, 126–127.

47 Ibid.,134.

49 Ibid., 136.

49 Ibid.

51 Matt Christopher, *On the Ice with Wayne Gretzky* (Boston: Little, Brown, 1997), 11.

54 *Ultimate Gretzky.*

59 Raber, *Wayne Gretzky*, 41.

61 Ibid., 44.

62 *Ultimate Gretzky.*

68 Gretzky, *Gretzky*, 227.

68 Raber, *Wayne Gretzky*, 9.

69 Ibid., 50.

72 Ibid., 54.

75 *Ultimate Gretzky.*

76 Ibid.

77 Ibid.

80 Russell Levine, "Gretzky Enters Hall with Trademark Selflessness," *NHL.com*, November 22, 1999 http://www.nhl.com/nhl/app ?service=page&page=NewsPage &articleid=279355 (September 28, 2006).

82 Scott Morrison, ed., *Wayne Gretzky: The Great Goodbye* (Toronto: Key Porter Books, 1999), 46.

84 Christopher, *On the Ice with Wayne Gretzky*, 133.

85 Morrison, 64.

88 *Ultimate Gretzky.*

88 Levine, "Gretzky Enters Hall with Trademark Selflessness."

89 "Gretzky Gets Star-Studded Farewell," *NHL.com*, April 18, 1999 http://www.nhl.com/history/ gretzky/041899gretzky.html (September 28, 2006).

90 Associated Press, "Hall of Fame Welcomes The Great One," *USA Today*, November 23, 1999 http://www.usatoday.com/sports/ hockey/gretzky/hall05.htm (September 28, 2006).

90 "Talking Gretzky," *NHL.com*, n.d. http://www.nhl.com/history/ gretzky/quotes.html (September 28, 2006).

93 ESPN.com News Service, "Gretzky Expected to Be Named Coyotes Coach Monday," *ESPN.com*, August 8, 2005 http://sports.espn.go.com/ nhl/news/story?id=2128012 (November 21, 2006).

94 Raber, *Wayne Gretzky*, 53.

95 CBC Sports, "What Happened to Team Canada?" *CBC.ca*, February 23, 2006 http://www.cbc.ca/olympics/sports/ icehockey/stories/index.shtml?/ story/olympics/national/2006/02/ 22/Sports/teamcanada-torino 060222.html (September 29, 2006).

95 "Talking Gretzky."

95–96 Associated Press, "Gretzky to Coach Coyotes for Next Five Seasons," May 31, 2006 http://sports.espn.go.com/ nhl/news/story?id=2464674 (September 29, 2006).

BIBLIOGRAPHY

Christopher, Matt. *On the Ice with Wayne Gretzky*. Boston: Little, Brown, 1997.

Foley, Mike. *Play-By-Play Hockey.* Minneapolis: Lerner Publications Company, 2000.

Gretzky, Wayne, with Rick Reilly. *Gretzky: An Autobiography.* New York: HarperCollins, 1990.

Hunter, Douglas. *Champions: The Illustrated History of Hockey's Greatest Dynasties.* Chicago: Triumph Books, 1997.

Leder, Jane Mersky. *Wayne Gretzky.* Mankato, MN: Crestwood House, 1985.

Morrison, Scott, ed. *Wayne Gretzky: The Great Goodbye.* Toronto: Key Porter Books, 1999.

Podnieks, Andrew. *The Great One: The Life and Times of Wayne Gretzky.* Chicago: Triumph Books, 1999.

Ultimate Gretzky 4-Disc Special Edition. DVD. Los Angeles, CA: Insight Sports Ltd., NHL Productions, Warner Home Video, 2006.

WEBSITES

NHL.com

http://www.nhl.com

The official site of the National Hockey League has scores, news, schedules, statistics, and much more.

Edmonton Oilers: The Official Site

http://www.edmontonoilers.com

The official site of the Edmonton Oilers offers updates on the team and its players and coaches and includes a history section.

Hockey Hall of Fame

http://www.hhof.com

The Hockey Hall of Fame's website includes information about the Hall and its inductees. Features include a virtual tour, photo galleries, and more.

Wayne Gretzky—The Official Homepage

http://www.waynegretzky.com

Wayne's official site includes news updates, photos, career statistics, information about Wayne's foundation, and more.

INDEX